FIN de SIECLE

'Miranda' by A.J. Gaskin (1862–1928) for *A Book of Fairy Tales* by
S. Baring Gould, 1894.

THE SAVOY

No. 1

January

1896

LEONARD SMITHERS

EFFINGHAM HOUSE
ARUNDEL STREET, STRAND
LONDON W.C.

AUBREY
BEARDSLEY.
1896.

Above Title-page by Aubrey Beardsley (1872–98) for *The Savoy*,
No. 1, January 1896.
Opposite Illustration by Hugh Thomson (1860–1920) for *Jack The
Giant Killer* (Macmillan), 1898. Pen and ink. 38 x 32 cm.
(SOTHEBY'S)

FIN de SIECLE
The Illustrators of the 'Nineties

THE HERALD ANNOUNCING THAT THUNDEL
WAS COME TO TAKE HIS REVENGE ON JACK.

by SIMON HOUFE

BARRIE & JENKINS
LONDON

IN MEMORY OF ROSALIE MANDER

First published in Great Britain in 1992
by Barrie & Jenkins Ltd., Random Century House,
20 Vauxhall Bridge Road, London SW1V 2SA

A catalogue record for this book is available from the British
Library

ISBN 0 7126 4540 3

Typeset by Rowlands Phototypesetting Ltd.,
Bury St Edmunds, Suffolk

Designed by David Fordham

Above
Page decoration by H. Granville Fell (1872–1951) for *Fairy Gifts*
in the Banbury Cross series (Dent), 1895.

Contents

This room with its books was Mr Keeling's secret romance; all his life, even from the days of the fish-shop, the collection of fine illustrated books had been his hobby, his *hortus inclusus*, where lay his escape from the eternal pursuit of money-making and from the tedium of domestic life. There he indulged his undeveloped love of the romance of literature, and the untutored joy with which design of line and colour inspired him. As an apostle of thoroughness in business and everything else, his books must be as well equipped as books could be: there must be fine bindings, the best paper and printing, and above all there must be pictures. When that was done you might say you had got a book. For rarity and antiquity he cared nothing at all: a sumptuous edition of a book of nursery rhymes was more desirable in his eyes than any Caxton.'

E. F. BENSON, *An Autumn Sowing*

Above
Page decoration by Laurence Housman (1865–1959) for *Jump to Glory Jane*, 1892.

Illustration by J.E. Southall (1861–1944) for *The Story of Blue-Beard*,
1895.

'In The Black Valley' by Heywood Sumner (1853–1940) for *Undine*
in the *English Illustrated Magazine*, 1887.

CHAPTER ONE

From the 'EIGHTIES to the 'NINETIES

In the spring of 1895, Max Beerbohm contributed an essay to the still youthful *Yellow Book*; it was simply called '1880'. This sparkling, frivolous piece of writing is typical of Max, lightsome, dandiacal and very tongue in cheek. It treats the year 1880 (only fifteen years before) as if it was some historical age and the figures who moved through it (mostly still alive) as if they were the heroes of an ancient Parnassus! It is true that Max himself was only eight at the time, but 1880 was nowhere near so remote and respected a year for him as he paints it here with mock nostalgia:

> Be it remembered that long before this time there had been in the heart of Chelsea a kind of cult of Beauty. Certain artists had settled there, deliberately refusing to work in the ordinary official way, and 'wrought', as they were wont to put it, 'for the pleasure and sake of all that is fair'. Swinburne, Morris, Rossetti, Whistler, Burne-Jones, were of this little community — all of them men of great industry and caring for little but their craft. Quietly and unbeknown they produced their poems or their pictures or their essays, read them or showed them to one another and worked on. In fact, Beauty had existed long before 1880. It was Mr Oscar Wilde who first trotted her round. This remarkable youth, a student at the University of Oxford, began to show himself everywhere, and even published a volume of poems in several editions as a kind of decoy to the shy artificers of Chelsea. The lampoons that at this period were written against him are still extant, and from them, and from the references to him in the contemporary journals, it would appear that it was to him that Art owed the great social vogue she enjoyed at this time.[1]

Beerbohm's witty, narcissistic gaze at his own coterie makes us chuckle, but there is a good deal of truth here about the origins of the 'Nineties and the *fin de siècle* in the decade that preceded it. He continues:

> Peacock feathers and sunflowers glittered in every room, the curio shops were ransacked for the furniture of Annish days, men and women, fired by the fervid words of the young Oscar, threw their mahogany into the streets. A few smart women even dressed themselves in suave draperies and unheard-of greens.[2]

These were the Aesthetic 'Eighties when a small circle of aesthetes ruled supremely on questions of taste and ridiculed those who transgressed. But the real difference that marked this earlier period of 'Art for Art's Sake' from the later one of the *fin de siècle* was a matter of degree rather than of style.

Perhaps the 'Eighties did appear as a glorious dawn to Max Beerbohm. They were certainly a kind of watershed for the new order, where titan figures had struggled over ideologies. William Morris and his Merton Abbey venture were struggling against the insidious machine, John Ruskin and James McNeill Whistler had fought in the witness box in November 1878, a confrontation of the old beliefs in improvement and self-help and the new creed of Art for Art's Sake and self-expression. The true dilettante remained above such squabbles but it was nevertheless rather interesting to him.

Following the exodus of French artists and writers to England in 1871, London had maintained its more cosmopolitan feel and had absorbed Continental habits. An increasing number of art students crossed to Parisian ateliers in the 1880s, furtive exhibitions of French paintings began to appear in the leading galleries, with even an occasional impressionist painting here and there. The manner in which literary and artistic society worked was also changing:

> The growth of London both in area and population had made some other public place of refreshment than the old chop house essential and the growing habit of dining in a restaurant was in itself a social revolution. The restaurant and the theatre and music hall prospered together. Thus the success of the Savoy operas caused the Savoy Hotel and Restaurant to come into being. The Lyceum under the princely domination of Henry Irving was the rage. The night houses of the 'sixties were turning into supper clubs and the music halls were becoming a folk institution where the events and characters of the day found a prompt celebration in song.[3]

It is quite significant that these eating places feature so strongly in the literature and art of the period. Critics like George Moore were drawn in them, Sickert was continually depicting them, Whistler, Wilde, Beerbohm, Frank Harris and Beardsley were their constant habitués. They are continually seen through the memoirs of the period as the places where illustrators met authors, where there was a flow of ideas and a greater fusion between graphic work and printed text than had been known previously. It is arguably one of the main factors that gave the art of the book such a high profile in the following decade.

Another reason for this happy marriage between visual interpretation and literary content, may have been the vogue in the 'Eighties for artist writers. William Blake was enjoying a revival, so too was Dante Gabriel Rosetti, dying of drugs but still lionised for his extraordinary power in poetry and image. William Morris certainly came into this category, with his astonishing capacity to inhabit the medieval mind in verse and prose,

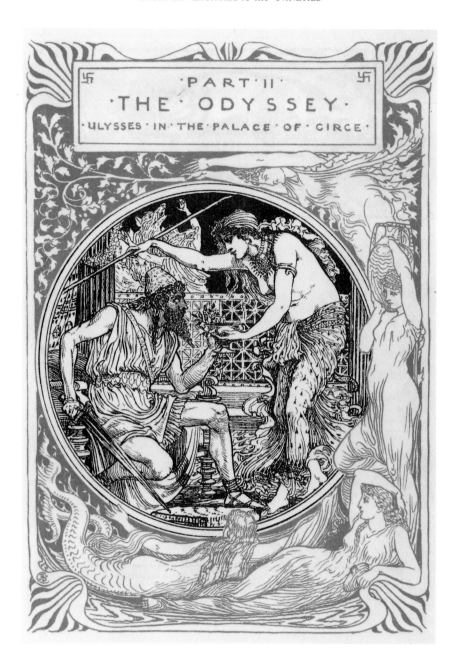

'Ulysses in the Palace of Circe' by Walter Crane (1845–1915) for
The Odyssey, 1887.

and to capture its spirit in ornament. To a lesser extent the poems of
William Bell Scott, the Northumbrian painter, were admired and among
the new generation of illustrators both Walter Crane and Kate Greenaway
drew for their own stories.

The Japanese craze which was an integral part of Aestheticism in the
1880s, and an important part of the 'new art' in the 'Nineties, was only
half understood by its many devotees. Whistler's long standing flirtation
with it dated back twenty years and was very influential, but even those
who modelled their work on the woodblock prints and their page designs

on Japanese typography, had no deep knowledge of the subject. William Rothenstein who arrived in Paris as a young student in 1889 found this mixture of the east with the west very alluring:

> The Japanese print cut across the sound French tradition of *la bonne peintre*, away from the luminous and nacreous handling of Chardin and Watteau. Most of us were seduced by this novelty, which, incidentally, led us away from the pursuit of form. We thought flat pictures more 'artistic' than solidly painted ones.[4]

Writing in 1896 Walter Crane expressed his doubts:

> We see unmistakeable traces of Japanese influences, however, almost everywhere — from the Parisian impressionist painter to the Japanese fan in the corner of the trade circulars, which shows it has been adopted as a stock printer's ornament. We see it in the sketchy blots and lines, and vignetted naturalistic flowers which are sometimes offered as page decorations, notably in American magazines and fashionable etchings. We have caught the vices of Japanese art certainly, even if we have assimilated some of the virtues.[5]

When considering the influence of page design, Crane was more enthusiastic:

> The fact that their text is written vertically, however, must be allowed for. This, indeed, converts their page into a panel, and their printed books become rather what we should consider sets of designs for decorating light panels, and extremely charming as such.

Crane also expresses approval for the 'dark border-line' that controls the page. This decorative scheme for the lay out of the page, the controlled border and the use of panels were all waiting to be discovered in the early 1880s. The wider public's conception of the Japanese influence was really confined to poor imitation ceramics and the production of W. S. Gilbert's *The Mikado* in 1885 which presented the philistine view in a rather engaging way.

In the Aesthetic 'Eighties, which Max Beerbohm observes from the heights of *The Yellow Book*, the sphere of influence was more limited. The clients of E. W. Godwin's houses and furniture were few and far between, the purchasers of Morris & Company's artefacts were in reality a privileged few, and there were scarcely any manuals or art magazines to inform the novice what was 'aesthetic' and what was not.[6] Only a few books reflected this phase, the 'Toy Books' of Crane and the 'greenery yallery' picture books of Kate Greenaway, which were influential on design.

The new apostles of Aestheticism were not particularly anxious to share their credo. Wilde and Whistler lectured in a patronising fashion, but Whistler in his *Ten o'clock Lecture*, characterised the artist as the last real aristocrat and the bourgeoisie as his sworn enemy. This was hardly music to the ears of publishers and editors, hoping to appeal to a vast middle-class, potentially art-loving readership! Within this charmed circle of the cognoscenti, there were rivalries too for the primacy of art over letters. This gave rise to Whistler's often quoted remark on Wilde. 'What has Oscar in common with Art? except that he dines at our tables and picks from our platters the plums for the puddings he peddles in the provinces. Oscar, the amiable, irresponsible esurient Oscar with no more sense of a picture than of the fit of a coat has the courage of the opinions . . . of others.'[7]

Punch successfully promoted the Aesthetic Movement by pillorying it. Just as with Leech's 'Bloomerism' thirty years earlier, *Punch* set up the 'culchah' of the aesthetes in order to knock it down, but in the process greatly expanded its notoriety. Du Maurier's creations of the painter, Maudle, and the poet, Jellaby Postlethwaite, were as popular as if the magazine had been running a series on Whistler and Wilde. Even Du Maurier's other invention, Mrs Cimabue Browne, belonged to an élite, a ridiculed one admittedly, but still a small exclusive circle of culture loving ladies. The most public persona of Aestheticism was 'Bunthorne', the ridiculous poet, based on Wilde, who was the principal character in Gilbert & Sullivan's *Patience*, produced at the Savoy Theatre in April 1881. The programme for the first night had a border of Crane-ish aesthetes and foilage, picked out in white against a dark background. The border also contained electric light bulbs which were used for the first time in an English theatre on this occasion. Ironically, the architects of Mr D'Oyly Carte's new theatre were Herbert Horne and Arthur Mackmurdo, two of the leading designers of the new art![8]

The new decade of the 'Nineties was to be rather different. The same personalities whom Max Beerbohm describes in his essay still stand in centre stage, the same indifference to middle-class values continues, but the new art was aimed at a wider public. It had suddenly become the age of mass communication, the period of poster art, the railway bookstall, the yellow back, the illustrated daily paper and the clever advertiser. Even *The Yellow Book* for which Max wrote his piece was not seriously 'exclusive' and went into many reprintings. The first volume had a print run of 7000 copies, the second volume 5000 copies; within twelve months they were in their fourth and third editions respectively. Almost without exception the subscription art magazines were more broadly based than their predecessors. The esoteric *Portfolio* (1871–93), and the high art *Magazine of Art* and *Art Journal* were replaced or transformed into more practical periodicals. The *Studio* was to cater for a completely new artistic readership of students and amateurs who entered for competitions, attended provincial exhibitions and yet regarded themselves as part of a European movement. It was probably the first time that book art, illustrations, covers, bindings or bookplates had been the subject of competitions, and more and more unknowns were trying to enter the field. Beardsley, one has to remember, made his début in the *Studio*. Even the cult of Japan, which had been so much the holy ground of 'Eighties aestheticism, was popularised by Samuel Bing's Parisian publication, *Japon Artistique* (1888–91), which appeared in a London edition in English. The Japonisme works of Octave Uzanne (1881–94) encouraged this refined taste; as one critic has put it, they were 'reflecting in their fastidious design the idea of the periodical itself as an art work'.[9]

The men of the 'Nineties saw their time as detached from the century, an interlude when only the few had the knowledge to discriminate. It was certainly a period of limited editions, but the editions were not always as limited as they appeared to be. John Lane, the leading publisher of the time, was a master of the special and the de luxe in his bookselling. His biographer set down how he could capture a market by means of hand-made paper, beautiful printing and untrimmed edges. 'Over and above the two hundred copies of the ordinary edition,' he writes of Le Gallienne's

Volumes in Folio, 'there are fifty copies on large paper. This was a conscious bid to titillate the appetite of the collector. Lane, if anyone, knew how to do that — knew how to stimulate desire where it already existed, and how to create it where it did not. Lane's strong point was his enthusiasm — I believe it was always real. It was infectious, irresistible.'[10] Lane's hugely popular *Keynotes Series* (1893), contained twenty-two volumes with covers and title-pages by Aubrey Beardsley selling at 3*s*.6*d*. each. Attractive little books, the volume by Florence Farr, *The Dancing Faun* (1894), had Whistler

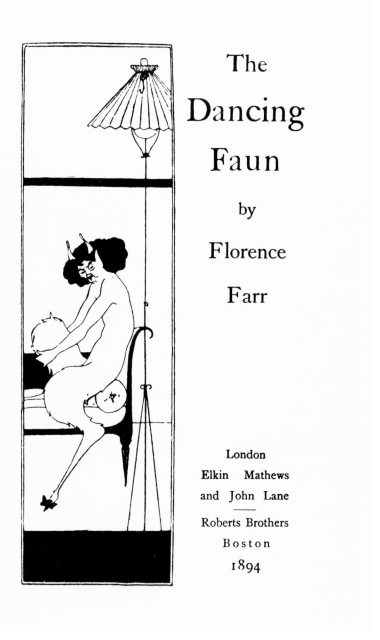

The

Dancing

Faun

by

Florence

Farr

London
Elkin   Mathews
and John Lane
———
Roberts Brothers
B o s t o n
1894

Frontispiece by Aubrey Beardsley (1872–98) for *The Dancing Faun*
by Florence Farr (Lane), 1894. The faun is a portrait of J. McNeil
Whistler.
(R. DE BEAUMONT COLLECTION)

CINDY.

WHEN Cinderella of great fame grew too old to care for dancing any more, she put her looking glass slippers away on the top top shelf of the top top attic of the house, and there they stayed until the great - great - great - great - great - grand - daughter Cindy found them. Now the fortunes of the House of Cinderella had fallen sadly, since great-and-the-rest grandmother Cin-

An 'aesthetic' page design by I.M.H.H. (identity unknown) for
'Cinderella' in *Five Trivial Tales*, (*c*.1885).
(R. DE BEAUMONT COLLECTION)

caricatured as a faun on cover and title. A nice touch for those who were in the know! But of course everyone was in the know. Lane's skill was to market such things to a wide public who still believed they were an artistic minority.

American influence was strong in both practice and approach from the early 1880s. American students in Paris were a potent force, but so too were the artists and illustrators working for the new style magazines such as *Harper's* and *Scribner's*. Joseph Pennell and Elizabeth Robins Pennell arrived in London in 1884 with the express purpose of writing and drawing for another American publication, the *Century*. American magazines democratised the art world by inventing the interview and the 'studio visit'. Suddenly the artist could not escape his public, and increasing coverage was given not only to academicians but also to the graphic artists and specialist illustrators. Throughout the 'Nineties, critics were knocking on studio doors and trying to prise out of the artist his personal preferences as well as his techniques. At no earlier moment could May or Beardsley, Pissarro or Nicholson, Furniss or Partridge have been so well known.

But the Aesthetic Movement of the 'Eighties had also been responsible for some remarkable experiments and these foreshadowed what was to come at the close of the century. The combination of the early Arts and Crafts movement with Aestheticism, brought together practical designers and idealistic theorists in a way that had not happened before. One of the first bodies to organise themselves in this way was the Century Guild. Founded in 1882 by Selwyn Image (1849–1930) and Charles Heygate Mackmurdo (1851–1942), the Guild was an exhibiting society that proclaimed 'the practical application of Art to life'. The *Century Guild Hobby Horse*, its organ from 1884, published a wide variety of articles on the arts as well as lists of approved craftsmen in many areas of the applied and decorative arts. It adhered very much to the practical philosophy of William Morris, but distanced itself from his socialism. Most important of all, it set a pattern for small circulation, carefully designed magazines, which was to affect their shape and content until the end of the Edwardian age. Mackmurdo was a brilliant designer of textiles and transferred his discoveries to the three dimensional realm of furniture as well as to the flat spaces of the printed page. He was able, like Morris, to find inspiration in plant form, but unlike that medievalising genius, he drew out their abstract structure for his own use. This first appears in the striking title-page for his book, *Wren's City Churches* (1883), where the flowers take on the sinuous contours of flames engulfing the title of the book.

The *Hobby Horse* had a similarly flowing title-page by Selwyn Image, although its forms were less abstracted and closer to traditional book design, because Image was a Ruskin pupil. The early numbers of the magazine had a considerable amount of Mackmurdo illustration or decoration, usually signed M.C.G. (Master Century Guild). With one artist and one aim, the numbers come across as a powerful unity, beautifully balanced as to letterpress, margins, and head and tailpieces. The latter are brilliant little examples of counterpoint, with their swirling lines or abstracted images flowing one way, only to be pulled back in another, like a sort of proto-*art nouveau* — which is indeed what they were to become. It is noticeable that the heroes of the *Hobby Horse* editors and designers are William Blake, whose illustrations they clearly imitate, the Old Masters and the Pre-Raphaelites. In Volume 2, 1886, they illustrate an early work of William Strang, and Image brings his pencil to bear on an 'In Memoriam' and a 'Christmas Carol'.

In the later issues, with the departure of Mackmurdo and the inclusion of Herbert Horne's work, the Whittingham Press become the printers and the character alters slightly. Horne's head and tail designs are decidedly more floreate in a literal sense, although not all the contributions are his.

Pencil drawing of a Christmas carol by Selwyn Image (1849–
1930). 5 ¾ x 3 ⅞ ins.
(AUTHOR'S COLLECTION)

Excellent work comes from Simeon Solomon and C. W. Whall. In addition,
the articles look back to the Renaissance (Horne was eventually to settle
in Florence) rather than to Blake and there are many illustrations of Flor-
entine incunabula. Despite this, the impact of the *Century Guild Hobby Horse*
was profound, providing that perfect example of artists working together
harmoniously and treating the printed page as a serious branch of fine art.

Frontispiece and title-page for *Sintram and His Companions* by Heywood Sumner (1853–1940), (Seeley Jackson & Halliday), 1883.

A lesser figure, but one with some influence, was the Arts and Crafts artist, Heywood Sumner (1853–1940). Sumner belongs to a tradition of country illustrating that has some of the lyricism of Samuel Palmer about it as well as the mysticism of a Blake. He was an early contributor to the *English Illustrated Magazine*, itself an important medium of change after it was founded in 1883. That year, Sumner designed the frontispiece, title-page and illustrations for *Sintram and His Companions*, a beautifully balanced composition which has in it some of the curvilinear patterns of early *art nouveau*. In 1887 he contributed some superb, mystical illustrations of *Undine* to the *English Illustrated Magazine*; these were published in book form in 1888. (See page *viii*)

All these seeds had borne rich fruit by the middle of the 'Nineties. There was such an explosion of interest in illustrative work, such a concentration of it in the journals and such a renaissance of it in the art schools, that some artists felt that this movement should be given a coherent form. Joseph Pennell, who had campaigned for the status of the illustrator since his arrival in London, now wished to form a body which would look after their interests. Pennell had briefly been Art Editor of the *Daily Chronicle* in an effort to present the best work of Whistler, Burne-Jones, Morris and Crane to a wider public. He then became Slade lecturer on illustration; as a result of this he undertook lecture tours up and down the country and linked the names of the famous with the names of outstanding students

Headpiece by Heywood Sumner (1853–1940) for the *English Illustrated Magazine*, 1887.

from the art schools. Pennell's Quakerish determination and American frontier attitudes would not let any opportunity slip!

The culmination of these efforts was the founding in 1894–5 of The Society of Illustrators. The Society was based on the group of aspiring draughtsmen who met from time to time in Pennell's Buckingham Street flat and was intended to be like the Society of Authors, protecting interests, defending rights and above all overseeing the vexed question of copyrights. Sir J. D. Linton became the president, Whistler, Seymour Haden and Holman Hunt vice-presidents, and F. W. Sullivan was secretary. The inaugural meeting, chaired by W. L. Thomas of the *Graphic* was not a success, but Pennell took over the meeting and eventually succeeded in getting 400 members at ten shillings and sixpence subscription per annum. Sullivan wrote, 'Perhaps the worst defect was that we had a Committee of twenty-five and a quorum of seven. There were regular monthly meetings and it was seldom that the same quorum attended. Hence there was no continuity of policy or effort and sometimes there was no quorum.'[11]

As the Society began to lose what little impetus it had, Pennell rather desperately proposed that they should combine together on a book. This became a London anthology known as *A London Garland*, and it remains the most tangible proof of the Society's efforts to give itself an identity, and of the 'Nineties' artists to originate a style from a vortex of influences. A handsome quarto with a vellum cover designed by Alfred Parsons, the volume says a great deal about the decade it was supposed to represent.

The veteran writer, W. E. Henley, was to edit the book, Macmillan were to publish it, and Pennell enlisted a formidable band of illustrators to contribute, including A. S. Hartrick, E. A. Abbey, Alfred Parsons, Raven Hill and Arthur Rackham. Henley was already at the centre of a circle of artists, writers and editors whom Max Beerbohm irreverently called 'The Henley Regatta'.

When the proofs were ready for *A London Garland*, Pennell and A. S. Hartrick went down to call on Henley at Barnes. Hartrick recalled the result: 'He looked at one or two unfavourable "duds" and in an instant turned on us like an enraged cockatoo, damned us up and down in that vocabulary both lurid and varied for which he was celebrated. He swore he would not allow his name to appear in such company etc. . . .'[12]

One can well understand why Henley was so dismissive and so curt in his preface to the book. While it has excellent things within its covers, particularly the headings of Robert Anning Bell and the etched 'Contents' page by E. A. Abbey, it is a diffuse and awkward hybrid. Despite the involvement of designers like Gleeson White, and perfectionists like Pennell, the book is a statement of what did not exist: coherence and shared interests among the illustrators of the *fin de siècle*. As Hartrick put it, 'so difficult is it to keep artists together'.[13]

All the schools and coteries are represented here (they will be discussed later in the book): the Pre-Raphaelites by Crane and Sandys; the realists by Hartrick, J. F. Sullivan and Paul Renouard; the 'Cranford' School by Henry Tonks, Rackham, E. J. Sullivan and Bernard Partridge; the French-inspired by J. W. T. Manuel and the new art by Beardsley. But Beardsley apart, there are no geniuses who capture the possibilities of the line block and half tone. In outstandingly good ink and wash, Raven Hill sets down the freedom of line of the 'Nineties in 'Sunday at Hampstead' and Walter Russell, later to be a Royal Academician, does the same with his brilliant 'Chamber in Grub Street', but these are exceptions. Jack B. Yeats' vignette is too small to attract attention, Edgar Wilson, creator of strange decorative patterns, contributes a stark Thames view and Beardsley's figure has had to be specially 'dressed' for the occasion in case it caused offence. Unlike Germany or Austria or even America, where some semblance of a style had stamped itself on the printed page, this country's work seemed very much at odds with itself. After 1895, the most unifying element was probably Beardsley; his forceful personality appears in every part of the art, exposing both its strengths and its weaknesses.

CHAPTER TWO

A GLANCE BACKWARDS

'We have come to the beginning of today rather than the end of yesterday, and can regard the "sixties" onwards as part of the present.'
GLEESON WHITE, 1897

The most perceptive art critic of the 'Nineties was Gleeson White (1853–98), who recognised more clearly than anyone else that the art of his decade did not stand alone, but had its roots in a grand tradition of draughtsmanship and professionalism. The younger artists of the 'Nineties were separated by little more than a generation from the great period of black-and-white illustration and as fashion changed more slowly then, the rising illustrators might eschew some artists of that school without rejecting the style. Of the great illustrators of the 1850s and 1860s, Rossetti and A. B. Houghton were dead, and Millais, Hughes and Holman Hunt were alive but not actively illustrating; only Burne-Jones and Walter Crane were still in the field. Joseph Pennell, in 1895, wrote: '. . . the three men who, in a great measure, are responsible for modern English illustration are working today: Birket Foster, Sir John Gilbert, and Harrison Weir, but, save the latter, they now produce scarcely any designs. Few of the brilliant band who succeeded them, however, are at work save Du Maurier and W. Small.'[1] Pennell's opinions were highly personal and one would not choose his selection of artists as the most influential, but all the names he mentions came to prominence in the 'Sixties or a little before.

Gleeson White's enthusiasm for the men of the 'Sixties has its culmination in the publication of his monumental *English Illustration 'The Sixties' 1857–70* (1897), which satisfied a need he had himself fostered. Here, once and for all, was a compendium of the famous illustrators of the time with a list of their most notable works, but also including the half-forgotten men and the ephemeral magazines for which they worked, and which were already collector's items. What Gleeson White does not say in his preface is that he had formed a very important library of the period on which his researches were based. He was perhaps the first man to create such a library. After his tragically early death, the library was put on the market by A. Lionel Isaacs in 1899; it included some 322 volumes featured in a specially printed catalogue. The introduction by Professor York Powell mentions the 'carefully chosen books' of 'Keene, Houghton, Pinwell, Watson, Walker, Hughes, Leighton, Lawson, Millais, Whistler, Solomon, Sandys, and a host of lesser lights . . .'.[2]

White's library and studio at 10 Theresa Terrace, Ravenscourt Park, London, were visited by many people from his wide circle of friends including visitors from the *Studio* magazine, the Art Workers Guild and the fields of publishing and design.[3] It is inconceivable that they would not have been privy to the remarkable library and the latest 'finds' among the illustrators; such championing would have been not only contagious but also widely influential. All the younger men of his day were represented in the modern section of his library and many of them spent congenial evenings in his company.

From the beginning of the *fin de siècle* years, the younger artists and writers were looking afresh at this work, and liking what they found. The intensity and emotion of the Rossettis and Millais in the *Moxon Tennyson* appealed to these new romantics; the fairyland of Arthur Hughes found echoes in the mystic jungle of the 'Nineties and the workmanlike frankness of the engraving endeared itself to the devotees of the Arts and Crafts Movement. It was a strange irony of the art world that within a few years of facsimile wood engraving being superseded, and within months of the Dalziel Brothers bankruptcy in 1893, the more progressive illustrators were turning their attention with nostalgic eyes to the wood engraved line. Just as the Pre-Raphaelite illustrators had collected woodcuts of the early sixteenth century, the late Victorian artist collector was being urged to assemble wood-engraved work of the 'Sixties with the idea of self-education. There was also some interest in the early woodcuts themselves, but in general the view of the Renaissance was taken through the prism of Pre-Raphaelitism. J. Lewis May recorded this transition of style in his youth: 'photogravure reproductions of Rossetti and Burne-Jones pictures were everywhere displacing Landseer'.[4]

What was markedly different about *this* revival was its distance from mere connoisseurship or collecting. Artists and publishers were in the forefront, keenly interested in reinvigorating the art of the present through the art of the past. The most dynamic of these enthusiasts was probably the aesthete, illustrator and designer Charles Ricketts (1866–1931) whose productive partnership with C. H. Shannon (1863–1937) had begun in 1882. By 1887, when scarcely past the student stage, they had adopted a code of life dedicated to art and by 1889 they were making a statement of their own beliefs in a privately issued magazine, the *Dial*. Although the first number of the magazine (there were to be five) was strongly influenced by the work of Gustave Moreau and Parisian symbolism, the second issue had a cover clearly derived from Rossetti and the woodcuts of Albrecht Dürer.

An older man like Gleeson White was likely to be influential and supportive of these revalued styles and some years later he wrote glowingly of Charles Ricketts in the *Pageant*, 1896, as well as explaining the sources of the revival: 'Quite recently we have welcomed the drawings by Sir Edward Burne-Jones, cut in wood for the Kelmscott Press editions, and here and there, both in England and on the Continent, are to be seen the first attempts at a new Renaissance of the Pre-Raphaelite idea, which, born in England, and peculiar to our country, is nevertheless still regarded as exotic, even by those who could so easily be better informed.'[5]

White accords Ricketts a prominent place in the movement, but goes on to explain convincingly how the strength of the 'Sixties illustrators had flickered out only to be revived by younger men:

> In 1870 the *Graphic* was started, and with it grew rapidly a new influence which, for a time at least, caused the Pre-Raphaelite ideal to be no more sought after. No longer was there even a desire to represent things with every possible circumstance, closely knit together in a design meant to be pleasant to the eye. In its stead, character in isolation was the ruling motive, with just enough actuality in the background to convey time. The pages of *Good Words* or *Once a Week* show this gradual change of front in men working simultaneously.[6]

This straightforward reporting, for that is what it was, characterised much of the work of the 'Seventies and early 'Eighties. As White recorded, the best men of the epoch 'contented themselves with a quiet effort to attain naturalistic effects without striving to keep their work intensely strained in its expression and full of spirituality.' But, he goes on, the Pre-Raphaelite style has always relied on 'a high degree of nervous tension' and this was where the change lay.[7]

Curiously enough, one of the great books of the 'Sixties style, *Dalziel's Bible Gallery*, lay dormant until its publication in 1881 and then was not fully appreciated for the magnificent work it was till some years later. So the seeds for a revival were widely scattered and it only remained for sensitive and enquiring minds like Charles Ricketts and Gleeson White, Joseph Pennell and Harry Quilter, Laurence Housman and G. S. Layard to grasp their importance for a new school. The *Century Guild Hobby Horse*, which in so many ways also led the field in the design and form of book art in the 1880s, also prompted the resurgence of interest in the 'Sixties School. As early as 1888 (Volume 12) there is an article on 'Frederick Sandys & The Woodcut Designers of Thirty Years Ago' by John Gray. This is the same Gray whom Rothenstein described as 'a fastidious young dandy and something of a poet'[8], whose *Silverpoints* had a cover designed by Ricketts and who was to become an intimate of Beardsley. All these men were waiting in the wings and their diversity of interest shows how closely intermixed were these many strands of influence.

Ricketts' inborn understanding of this tradition greatly enhanced its progress, for he was not only a dynamic designer and innovator, but a powerful voice in proselytizing and educating. The Vale Press, which he founded in 1894, had a West End shop and in its gallery were held exhibitions of Millais, A. B. Houghton and Renaissance woodcuts in an effort to stimulate public awareness of fine illustration. In 1895 they showed 40 designs by A. B. Houghton 'Including Original Drawings and Proofs Retouched By The Artist'. In the catalogue preface, C. J. Holmes wrote: 'In Houghton's work, two things strike us repeatedly, when we see it adequately today; its mastery of technique and style, and its temperament: the mastery so swift and spontaneous, so lavish of its audacities, so noble in its economies; the temperament so dramatic, so passionate, so satiric, and so witty.'[9] Small wonder that such fire appealed to younger artists in a lack-lustre period! In 1898 there was a similar show devoted to Millais which included thirty-two woodcuts from the *Moxon Tennyson*, *Good Words*, *Punch* and the *Cornhill*. Holmes again wrote a laudatory preface for the

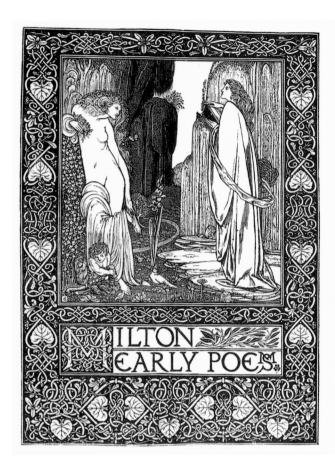

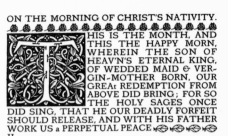

ON THE MORNING OF CHRIST'S NATIVITY.

HIS IS THE MONTH, AND THIS THE HAPPY MORN, WHEREIN THE SON OF HEAV'N'S ETERNAL KING, OF WEDDED MAID & VER-GIN-MOTHER BORN, OUR GREAt REDEMPTION FROM ABOVE DID BRING; FOR SO THE HOLY SAGES ONCE DID SING, THAT HE OUR DEADLY FORFEIT SHOULD RELEASE, AND WITH HIS FATHER WORK US a PERPETUAL PEACE

II.
THAT GLORIOUS FORM, That LIGHT INSUFF-ERABLE, AND THAT FAR-BEAMING BLAZE of MAJESTY,WHERWITH HE WONT at HEAV'N'S HIGH COUNCEL TABLE TO SIT THE MIDST of TRINALUNITY, HE LAID ASIDE; &, HERE with US TO BE, FORSOOK THE COURTS OF EVER-LASTING DAY, & CHOSE WITH US A DARK-SOME HOUSE of MORTAL CLAY

III.
SAY, HEAV'NLY MUSE, SHALL NOT THY SA-CRED VEIN AFFORD A PRESENT TO THE IN-FANT GOD / HAST THOU NO VERSE, NO HYMN, OR SOLEMN STREIN, TO WELCOME HIM to THIS HIS NEW ABODE, NOW, WHILE THE HEAV'N BY THE SUNS TEAM UNTROD, HATH TOOK NO PRINT OF THE APPROACH-ING LIGHT, & ALL THE SPANGLED HOST KEEP WATCH IN SQUADRONS BRIGHT /

iii   a   See

Frontispiece and first page by Charles Ricketts (1866–1931) for
The Early Poems of John Milton (The Vale Press), 1896.
(SOTHEBY'S)

recently deceased President of the Royal Academy: 'in all round accom-plishment Menzel alone can compete with him'.[10] Two further exhibitions in 1898 included 'Famous Woodcut Illustrations of the Fifteenth & Early Sixteenth Centuries' and an exhibition of accepted contemporaries: Rick-etts and Shannon of course, but also Reginald Savage, T. S. Moore,

Headpiece for the *Dial* by Charles Ricketts (1866–1931).

'Phedra and Ariadne' by Charles Ricketts (1866–1931) for the *Dial*,
1892. Pen and ink.

Alphonse Legros and William Nicholson. This brought the tradition up to
date and demonstrated its continuity in the eyes of the visiting public.

Ricketts' clearest essays in this style remain the early numbers of the
Dial where he was his own master and could personally supervise the best
synthesis of his press and his circle. The debt is implicit in the early
numbers but the decoration owes more perhaps to Burne-Jones than to
the first Pre-Raphaelite illustrators.

'Solitude' by Lucien Pissarro (1863–1944) for the *Dial*, 1893.
Wood-engraving.

Its early appearance was unusual in being so carefully designed with
Ricketts' headings and a large frontispiece of 'Bethemoth' by Reginald
Savage which was noticed with enthusiasm by the young Charles Holme.
There is also a healthy amateurism in the notes that appear from time to
time in the magazine such as: 'We would Thank TSM and HJR Whose
Timely Aid Made Possible The Publication of This Number of *The Dial*'.
There was also a rather unbusiness-like approach to the distribution. Laur-
ence Housman himself had difficulty obtaining a copy and in any case
No. 2, published in 1892, was limited to two hundred copies.

The 1893 issue, No. 3, had the novelty of a frontispiece by Savage,
'Centaurs', printed in green and another wood engraving by Sturge Moore,
'Pan Mountain', printed in the same colour. The highlight of this number,
however, was probably Ricketts' superb early ink drawing, 'Phedra and
Ariadne', which seems to owe such a lot not only to the influence of
Burne-Jones, but also to the Paris artists that were so admired by Ricketts
and Shannon. This issue also shows the artists of the Vale Press running
in tandem with Lucien Pissarro (represented by the print 'Solitude').

'December' by Charles Shannon (1863–1937) for the *Dial*, 1897.
Woodcut.
'Vision of James I of Scotland' by T. Sturge Moore (1871–1944)
for the *Dial*, 1897. Woodcut.

There was then a three-year gap before the *Dial* No. 4 appeared in 1896 with lithographs and silverpoints by Shannon, two illustrations to 'The King's Quair' by Ricketts and 'Le Petit Chapeau Rouge' by Pissarro. The fifth and last number for 1897 contains a striking woodcut, 'December', by Shannon, which is at once powerful and decorative, and Sturge Moore's weird 'Vision of King James I', which has that artist's angular mannerisms. But in another book, produced commercially but printed in a limited edition, *Poems Dramatic and Lyrical* by Lord De Tabley (1893), the woodcut illustrations are conceived in an unequivocal Rossettian style. This is particularly apparent in 'The Two Old Kings' where the figures seem confined in the picture space, with the Pre-Raphaelite convention of an open window above, and similarly in the highly decorative 'The Knight in the Wood' and the Düreresque 'The Defeat of Glory'. The first two approximate most forcibly with the illustrations in the *Moxon Tennyson* of 1857, in particular the much admired 'Palace of Art'. Freemantle & Co, realising that the time was ripe, were preparing to re-issue the Moxon with an introduction by Joseph Pennell. This finally appeared in 1901. In his introduction, Pennell mentions how gradually the work of the 'Sixties began to affect the art of the new men:

> Illustrators of the 'Nineties working according to the new conditions, occasionally, somehow, referred to an old number of the 'Graphic', or an odd volume of 'Once a Week' picked up from a twopenny box at a bookstall. This set them to study more systematically other work of the period. They began to talk about it. People began to remember vaguely that they had been brought up on these very illustrations in their childhood. The thing was in the air, until now, as I have said, the fact of the importance of the 'Black and White' of forty years ago is fully recognised by a few people.[11]

'The Lost Piece of Silver' by Charles Ricketts (1866–1931) for
Parables From The Gospels (Hacon and Ricketts), 1903. Wood-
engraving.

A slightly later but equally important group of illustrations, suggestive
of the 1860s, are in *The Parables from the Gospels* (1903), published by Hacon
and Ricketts at the Vale Press. The ten exquisite woodcuts by Ricketts
invite comparison at once with Millais' *Parables* of 1863, though their small
scale and simple surroundings also suggest the kind of sixteenth-century
typographical work that the artist admired.

His respect for Millais was not limited to this elegant tribute. In the
Pageant (1896), a Christmas gift-book edited by Gleeson White and C. H.
Shannon, in which Ricketts was also involved, two important Millais works
were illustrated. This volume also included two works by Burne-Jones
and the remarkable drawing of 'The Magdalene at the House of Simon
the Pharisee' by D. G. Rossetti which Ricketts had recently found in a
junk shop.

Ricketts was far too creative an individual to be set in this mould for
long, but other artists followed his lead and adopted a manner of illustration
which took its cue from the woodcut or the wood-engraved line, though
it was drawn entirely in pen and ink. Almost all of these artists came into

contact at some time with Ricketts and Shannon, or their disciples, forming a very definite coterie that associated with each other and admired many of the same things.

Laurence Housman (1865–1959) was one of the most gifted of these artists although his career as an illustrator was short. He and his sister, the wood-engraver Clemence Housman, who were working at Kennington Art School, also joined the Miller's Lane School in South Lambeth. Wood-engraving was still taught at the school and there they came into contact with fellow students, Ricketts and Shannon. Housman was both author and artist, and as the editor of a Blake book for Kegan Paul in 1893 he already had 'a dim sense that Blake was one of the greatest English artists.'[12] It was by way of Blake, a Pre-Raphaelite enthusiasm, that Housman came to the illustrators of the 'Sixties and in particular that most fluent of draughtsmen, Arthur Boyd Houghton. The discovery of Houghton must

"*Justice, my lord governor, justice! Woe is me! he has robbed me of what I have kept above these three and twenty years.*"

'Justice' by A. Boyd Houghton (1836–75) for *Don Quixote*, 1865.
Wood-engraving.

have been something of a revelation to Housman, particularly as his appreciation came through looking at his original drawings, preserved by his daughter. Housman realised at once that though the debt to Pre-Raphaelitism was still intrinsic to the work, this second generation of artists had a new vitality about them and a fresher contact with life and naturalism. Other artists of the school fell into sentimentality, but 'Houghton alone worked out a mastery in style compatible with an extreme realism of treatment'.[13]

Housman's 1895 essay on Houghton, 'A Forgotten Book Illustrator', in *Bibliographica* became the book, *Arthur Boyd Houghton: A Selection From His Work*, published in 1896. As well as showing the original drawings, it illustrated numerous examples from Houghton's 1863–5 masterpiece, *The Arabian Nights*, in which the artist demonstrated the full vigour of his draughtsmanship and the extraordinary detail of his observation. Houghton's range includes legendary illustration, domestic scenes and his stirring reporting of American life for the *Graphic*. His dexterity and frankness were a double-edged sword; he was both outstanding and controversial. Housman wrote: 'Among artists, and those who care at all deeply for the great things of art, he cannot be forgotten: for them his work is at once too much an influence and a problem.'[14]

Influence it certainly was, and Housman's championship of the artist must have gone a long way to make him the most copied illustrator after Rossetti and Millais in the 1890s. A. S. Hartrick, in particular, mentions that he copied Houghton's work from among others in the early volumes of the *Graphic*[15] in much the same way that C. J. Holmes was copying Keene engravings of the 'Sixties in the Art Library, South Kensington.[16]

Housman's early work had consisted of Pre-Raphaelitish contributions to *The Universal Review* in 1890, edited by that arch enthusiast for the 'Sixties, Harry Quilter, as well as to *Atalanta* in 1892. Contact with Charles Ricketts disciplined and chanelled these vague yearnings. 'Within a month,' Housman recalled, 'Ricketts had dragged me away from my timid preference for fuzzy chalk drawing, as a means of concealing my bad draughtsmanship, and had set me to pen-work, with Rossetti and the other pre-Raphaelites as my main guides both in composition and technique. From that time on, I felt set—I acquired a new confidence; I had found out at last what I wanted to do.'[17]

Housman was virtually unique among the prime illustrators of the 'Nineties in being a poet and prose writer as well as a draughtsman, and even more unusual in working so closely with his engraver sister, to whom one of his books is dedicated. This personal devotion seems to mark out the books, endowing the black-and-white work with a kind of spiritual element reminiscent of Blake. This ascetic dedication to art was not unlike that of Ricketts and Shannon, Housman explained it simply: '. . . my indifference to a paying popularity has, I believe, in the long run helped and not hindered my output of the things which semed to me most worth doing.'[18]

He first came to prominence in an unusual book for Swann-Sonnenschein in 1892, George Meredith's *Jump to Glory Jane*. In this personally designed book, Housman not only contributed the forty-four designs but also produced his own script for the ballad, a rather Blakean innovation. Some of the drawings already look to A. B. Houghton's illustrations, but even more have echoes of the rural illustrations of that group of

'A Revelation came on Jane' by Laurence Housman (1865–1959)
for *Jump to Glory Jane* by George Meredith, 1892.

G. J. Pinwell and Fred Walker, particularly the plate of Jane receiving
her revelation. (See page *vi*)

The book most often cited as being close in feeling to the Pre-
Raphaelites, and certainly Housman's masterpiece, is the 1893 edition of
Christina Rossetti's *Goblin Market*, originally illustrated by Rossetti himself.

This was also very much a 'complete' Housman book, the fashionable 'Nineties size of tall octavo had a repeating floral pattern blocked in gold on green on the cover and more than forty text, page and double page illustrations by the artist. Lord Leighton acquired the original drawing of the frontispiece and particularly commended the artist for the decorative quality of the production, 'the combination of figures with decoration'.[19] The daring double page spread (pp. 15–16) is a veritable tour de force, the central figure of the woman in the left-hand page relating directly to the figure in 'The Parable of the Leaven' in Millais' *Parables*. The Goblin figures are strangely reminiscent of Doyle. This book was also printed in a special large paper edition of 500 copies but seems much less *fin de siècle* than its smaller counterpart.

The series of books written, designed and illustrated by Housman between 1894 and 1900 are the quintessence of the best 'Nineties romanti-

Page opening by Laurence Housman (1865–1959) for *Goblin Market*
by Christina Rossetti, 1893.

'The Leaven' by Sir John Millais (1829–96) for *The Parables*, 1864.
Wood-engraving.

cism. All these books are superb in format and detail, quietly manneristic but with none of the excesses of the star performers. They hark back to the wood-engraved line of the 1860s but remain, nevertheless, creations of their time. *A Farm in Fairyland* (1894), *The House of Joy* (1895), *Green Arras* (1896), *All Fellows* (1896), *The Field of Clover* (1898) and *The Little Land* (1899) are all full of highly individual things. The frontispieces are carefully wrought in the manner of the Vale books, with interlacing, densely packed Celtic motifs for *The House of Joy* and a richer, darker, more Renaissance strain for *The Field of Clover*. Ricketts' influence seems to be dominant, but it is quite possible that Housman's inventiveness may have been reciprocal.

A paradox is the underlying ambiguity in a number of the illustrations. Some in *The House of Joy* and *The Field of Clover* are notoriously difficult to

Frontispiece and title-page by Laurence Housman (1865–1959) for
The House of Joy, 1895.

decipher: 'The Burning Rose' in the latter book, for example, is a riot of
figures and tousled hair and a strange dream quality subsists in the same
book's 'The Feeding of the Emigrants'. Both pages owe something to the
Moxon Tennyson and the works of Holman Hunt and Rossetti, but strangely
enough the most popular artists of the 'Sixties, Houghton and Millais,
were distinguished by great clarity of line.

This sense of uncertainty and of the numinous, in which reality and
fantasy are exchanged or move rapidly from the one to the other, must have
been intentional. Housman was fascinated by shapes and the possibilities of
chance. In a copy of a later book, *The Blue Moon* (1904), in a private
collection, he has pasted in a photograph which inspired a full-page illustration. The artist had seen the photograph upside down and been alerted to
the compositional possibilities of its shapes. Working from these random
juxtapositions, he has built up a pattern that serves his purpose. This
dimension of serendipity in illustrating a text (admittedly his own text)
seems to have intrigued the artist and may well have been an element in
the earlier books.

Housman's real understanding of the earlier artists can be gauged by
remarks he made twenty-five years later:

Frontispiece and title-page by Laurence Housman (1865–1959) for
The Field of Clover, 1898.

In Pre-Raphaelite pictures, closely grouped faces and hands have a
new and vigorous significance; and the figures are generally arrested,
brought to a standstill by some appeal to the emotions, often as though
they were trying deeply to read each other's thoughts. The forces born
of an emotional conflict (holding the body in arrest) have passed into
the face; and though some slight exceptions occur, it will be found
that the central interest of picture after picture, produced while Pre-
Raphaelitism was at its real heat, consists in the exchanged regards of
friends and lovers, or in the strong restrained pose from which all
gesticulation is banished, or even in the deeply-divined expression of
a single face.[20]

That Housman was capable of identifying with this literary intuition is
apparent in all his illustrations of books in the 'Nineties.

Housman's literary achievements and poor eyesight meant that his
career as book illustrator ended shortly after the turn of the century A
critic in the *Pall Mall Gazette* was able to write of *Green Arras*, 'His poems
are as original as his drawings, and possess the same fine charm . . .' It
was singular praise even in the 1890s.

Another artist very closely associated with Ricketts and Shannon, and a devotee of the Golden Age, was Reginald Savage (*fl.* 1886–1933). He was an illustrator and pen draughtsman of high quality, contributing to the *Dial* and the *Pageant* and doing a great deal of work for C. R. Ashbee's Essex House Press. Ashbee wrote of him, 'He has in his work that feeling of tapestry and stained glass without colour which the woodcut designer is ever searching for: he has also a very subtle and delicate sense of humour.' His 1896 contribution to the *Pageant* was an illustration of Wilhelm Meinhold's horrific story, *Sidonia Von Bork*, which had been popular with the Pre-Raphaelites and was enjoying a revival. He took as his subject 'Sidonia and Otto von Bork on the Waterway to Stettin' which was to accompany an article on Meinhold by Professor York Powell. Savage's brilliant, crowded pen drawing has the same tensions we have seen in Housman, but the line is more distinct and the overall woodcut effect clearer. Like so many of this circle, Savage has familiarised himself with the woodcuts of Dürer, packing in details and events with the eye of a weaver. It is an extraordinary achievement in such a restricted area and its merits soon caught the eye of the Victorian collector, Pickford Waller, who acquired it for his home. Further on in the volume, Savage illustrated 'The Albatross' from Coleridge's *Ancient Mariner*.

In 1897, Savage contributed another minor masterpiece to the *Pageant*, also based on the Coleridge poem. This is peculiarly reminiscent of Ros-

'Sidonia and Otto von Bork on the Waterway to Stettin' by Reginald
Savage (*fl.* 1886–1933). Pen and ink. Signed. 1896. 5 ½ x 7 ½ ins.

'The Albatross' by Reginald Savage (*fl.* 1886–1933) for the *Pageant*,
1896.

setti's *Moxon Tennyson* work in such pages as the second 'Lady of Shallott'
illustration and his 'Sir Galahad'. The tense figures of the Ancient Mariner
and the wedding guests are pressed into the confined picture space with
claustrophobic results and yet beyond is a sunlit and empty harbour. With
such contrasts, artists like Savage generated emotion, passion and interest
in a square of only a few inches. It is small wonder that Housman could
say of Coleridge's epic poem, 'I do not think one can be wrong in saying
that "The Ancient Mariner" and all it stood for was one of the moving
forces behind Pre-Raphaelitism.'[21] The artist's other published work, *The
Journal of John Woolman* (1901), *Pilgrim's Progress*, *The Poems of William
Shakespeare* (1899), all for the Essex House Press, are marked, as one
would expect, by more of an Arts and Crafts influence. Walter Crane
particularly noted 'the weird designs' of Savage's pen.[22]

It would be appropriate here to mention the name of Thomas Sturge
Moore (1870–1944), who was also an associate of Ricketts. Sturge Moore
was the latter's friend, executor and memorialiser and lived with the two
artists at the Vale. He had studied with Shannon at Croydon and Ricketts
at Lambeth, specialising in wood-engraving, and taking as his inspiration
the work of Blake, Calvert and the German little masters, rather than the
1860s School. He had only published about fifteen wood engravings before
1900, although he exhibited some at the Van Wisselingh Gallery in 1898.

Of Gilderoy sae fraid they were,
    They bound him mickle strong.
Tull Edenburrow they led him thair,
    And on a gallows hung:
They hung him high aboon the rest,
    He was sae trim a boy;
Thair dyed the youth whom I lued best,
    My handsome Gilderoy.

88

Illustration by Reginald Savage (*fl.* 1886–1933) for *A Book of Romantic Ballads*, 1901.

He was later associated with the Eragny Press and designed competent book covers in the 1920s and later. Like Housman, he was both artist and writer and, like so many of those he admired, basically a literary figure. His few contributions to the *Dial* are strangely mannered creations, almost precursors of Gill.

Among the major figures of this decade who were influenced by the 1860s, mention must be made of Henry Ospovat (1877–1909), although he died young and his output was relatively small. Ospovat was born in Russia but he emigrated to England with his family and studied, from 1893 to 1897, at the Manchester School of Art where he was influenced by Walter Crane. At the Royal College of Art in 1897 he came under the

'All these I better in one general best. . .' by Henry Ospovat (1877–
1909) for *Shakespeare's Sonnets*, 1899.
'So it is not with me as with that Muse' by Henry Ospovat (1877–
1909) for *Shakespeare's Sonnets*, 1899.

influence of T. R. Way, Whistler's lithographer, a tenuous connection with
the earlier artists.[23] Like all the younger artists, perhaps because so many
of them were strongly literary, the main influence seems to have been
D. G. Rossetti. *Shakespeare's Sonnets*, issued by John Lane in 1899, is a
charming little book, well designed and printed with nine full-page illustrations as well as a frontispiece, title-page and decorations. Where Savage's
work was so refined, Ospovat's is much broader in content and execution,
the treatment more powerful and sensuous, the figures less introspective.
His drawings for illustration (in a private collection) show a similar sweep
of chalk or pen; he was more interested in projecting the book in a painterly
way than in simply imitating the wood engraving. Until then he had been
concentrating on book-plate design in the Birmingham School style and
studying the work of Rossetti, Sandys and Houghton. Although not principally a book decorator, he knew how to decorate a book, a fact that is
abundantly clear in his next production, *Poems By Matthew Arnold*, published
by Lane in 1900. This shows a great advance: the artist has the measure
of his subject, the scope is wider and the book decorations are conceived in
a bolder and more individual style. The frontispiece is a strongly decorative
image of the 1860s, with the falling hair of the 'Duchess Marguerite',
and the play of gathered folds in her heavy gown epitomising torrid,
Pre-Raphaelite medievalism. But the influences do not come solely from

'The Forsaken Merman' by Henry Ospovat (1877–1909) for *Poems*
by Matthew Arnold, 1900.

this direction: some of the headings have more of international *art nouveau*
or symbolism, about them, and some of the figures have more than a
hint of Ospovat's forceful contemporary, E. J. Sullivan. His heading, 'To
Fausta', has a Ricketts rhythm in the curving lines but there no personal
connection with the artist is recorded. The outstanding contributions are
the illustrations of the 'Scholar Gypsy', where Ospovat seems to find his
melancholy self in the full-page drawing. His earliest biographer says, 'The
poem itself suggests nothing half so still and grave.'[24] Later illustrations to
Shakespeare (1901) continue this advance towards maturity, but Ospovat's

last years seem to have been marked by his virtuoso caricatures and portraits unconnected to books. It is not, I think, fanciful to see, in the vein
of self-absorbed brooding in Ospovat's book work, a specially Russian
dimension.

A very young and aspiring artist was Paul Woodroffe (1875–1954),
whose Roman Catholic upbringing led him into the paths of religious book
illustration and stained glass design, as well as pictures and decoration for
romantic fiction and children's books. His *Ye Booke of Nursery Rhymes* (1895)
is remarkable, considering that it was the work of a Slade student of twenty
years of age; it combines both attractive drawing and very well organised

'How St Benet made a broken sieve whole' by Paul Woodroffe
(1875–1945) for *The Little Flowers of St Benet*, 1901.

33

decoration. In 1896 he produced some modest headpieces for the *Quarto* and a rather ordinary 'Nativity' in a woodcut style. In the next four or five years some very interesting work came from his pen, notably *The Second Book of Nursery Rhymes* (1896), *The Little Flowers of St Francis* (1899), *The Confessions of St Augustine* (1900) and *The Little Flowers of St Benet* (1901). Some of these fine illustrated books have a distinct feel of the 'Sixties and indeed of Housman, whom Woodroffe had met through Clemence Housman.[25] But Woodroffe's true home was to be found in the Arts and Crafts Movement , as is clear from his great facility in designing bindings and composing decorative motifs with an almost architectural understanding. He joined the stained glass artist Christopher Whall in the 1890s and was later associated with C. R. Ashbee.

A considerable number of illustrators continued the idiom of the 'Sixties well into the next century, and a few of the younger ones are worth considering in this context. One of the best series of illustrated books was issued by John Lane as 'Flowers of Parnassus', small artistic pocket books (cloth 1*s*. and leather 1*s*.6*d*.), described as 'Famous Poems Illustrated'. By 1902 there were fourteen titles advertised, the most significant new illustrators being Herbert Cole and Philip Connard, although Lane reissued some Beardsley *Rape of The Lock* illustrations in this format.

Herbert Cole (1867–1931) is a delightful but little known illustrator of this period. For Lane he illustrated *The Nut-Brown Maid* by F. B. Money Coutts (1901), *A Ballade upon a Wedding* by Sir John Suckling (1901), *Rubaiyat of Omar Khayyam* translated by Edward Fitzgerald (1905) and *Christmas at the Mermaid* by Watts Dunton (undated). Cole was teaching illustration at the Camberwell School of Art at about this time and was influenced by Walter Crane and Rossetti.[26] In an appreciation of Cole, E. J. Sullivan wrote, 'it was easy to trace many of his admirations and interests: Watts, Burne-Jones, C. H. Shannon, and Greiffenhagen all showing an occasional direct influence'.[27] Some of the illustrations to *The Nut-Brown Maid* have a strong feeling of Rossetti and the degree of intensity associated with the *Moxon*. The last illustration in this diminutive volume, 'For you have won a baron's son . . .', has the combination of window seat and costumed figures that instantly recall it. His *Ancient Mariner* (1900) and *Gulliver's Travels*, the same year, show a lighter picture book style.

Also outstanding in this series was the work of Philip Connard R.A. (1875–1958) who had a slight career as an illustrator before becoming a distinguished portrait painter. His *Marpessa* by Stephen Phillips is very much in the spirit of the *fin de siècle*, containing illustrations and decorations of great delicacy, which are gentler in mood than much turn-of-the-century work. Of particular merit are his frontispiece 'Roaming with morning thoughts . . .', the very 'Sixties 'The fierce ingratitude of children loved' and the idyllic 'He shall give me passionate children'. The rustic idyll of these have something of Housman in them, but the extraordinary tour de force of 'More tender tasks to steal upon the sea' is worthy of Ricketts through being both powerful and decorative. Connard also illustrated Browning's *The Statue and The Bust* in this series. Other artists contributing were Percy Bulcock, Amelia Bauerle and F. L. Griggs, but with less obvious stylistic debts to the past.

The tradition was certainly carried forward by Byam Shaw (1872–1919), well known for his stylish narrative watercolours in a Rossettian

For you have won a baron's son, and not a banished man.

'For you have won a baron's son . . .' by Herbert Cole (1867–1931)
for *The Nut Brown Maid*, 1901.

vein. Shaw was very prolific and imaginative, covering the areas of stained
glass, tapestry and stage design, but in the 1890s he was best known for
set-piece watercolours and illustrations. For George Allen Shaw illustrated
Tales From Bocaccio (1899), a charming early book with twenty black-and-
white drawings of characteristic deftness and accuracy. When he came to
illustrate Charles Reade's *The Cloister and the Hearth* (1909), Shaw contributed work with the same clarity of line observable in 'Sixties engravings.
Unfortunately, in capturing the feeling of an earlier style, some publishers
went too far. Messrs Bell, in publishing his *Browning* in 1897, left him
'much troubled at finding that the original drawings had lost some of their
finer qualities, owing to too rough paper having having been chosen for
the illustrated page'.[28] Generally, however, he belongs to the Edwardians
and the colour plate book.

A friend and contemporary of Byam Shaw was Eleanor Fortescue
Brickdale (1872–1945). She spans the two epochs of the 1890s and the
1900s: the period when black-and-white work was predominant, and that
when colour illustration gained the upper hand. Trained at the Royal

'The Princess's Pets' by J. Byam Shaw (1873–1919). Pen and ink
drawing for unidentified illustration, 1901.
(SOTHEBY'S)

Academy, she was illustrating *Ivanhoe* for G. Bell & Sons as early as 1899.
She was championed by Byam Shaw's wife in a *Studio* article, which is not
surprising since her elaborate historical and literary themes were akin to
his. She was noted for accurate if rather overworked period detail, a strong
decorative sense and gorgeous colour in the treatment of sweeping robes
and rich interiors. Her great period of success was after 1906 when she
produced lavish watercolour illustrations for the gift-books of Messrs
Methuen and Chatto & Windus.

The idea that this return to the past was simply a London-based trend
is contradicted by the work of Clinton Balmer (*fl.* 1901–22). He was a
Liverpool artist who studied under Augustus John and seems to have been
inspired by Ricketts' and Shannon's work, presumably from the books that
came his way. It is very much an 'aesthetic' style, but perfect for his one
important book, *The Gate of Smaragdas*, by Gordon Bottomley, who had
befriended him. The volume is dated 1904, but the arrangement of text
and plates has a 'Nineties feel and was praised by Ricketts, Shannon and
Yeats. Printed at Ulverston, the book then had a sheet inserted stating
'The First and Sole Publisher of This Book is Elkin Mathews Vigo Street
London W. 1904'.

In 1901 the Victoria and Albert Museum held an important exhibition of Modern Illustration with a sizeable section devoted to the 'Golden Age'. This was a fitting end to the years that had seen such a revival and had witnessed major biographies published on G. J. Pinwell, Fred Walker and Keene. J. M. Bulloch, writing in the Special Winter Number of the *Studio* (1900–1), which covered the exhibition, voiced some misgivings. But he did conclude by saying, 'for those who lament the vanishing woodcut there is ample compensation in the pen-work of today, for the creator himself can now give us the additional personality which the intermediary of another day, the wood engraver, was compelled to impart, in virtue of his very entity, however small that may have been'.[29]

Illustration by Clinton Balmer (*fl.* 1901–22)˙ for *The Gate of Smaragdus*, 1904.

HEERE BIGYNNETH THE PRIORESSES TALE

WAS IN ASYE, IN A GREET CITEE,
Amonges cristene folk, a Jewerye,
Sustened by a lord of that contree
for foule usure, and lucre of vileynye,
Hateful to Crist and to his compaignye;
And thurgh the strete men myghte ride or wende,
for it was free, and open at eyther ende.

A litel scole of cristen folk ther stood
Doun at the ferther ende, in which ther were
Children an heepe, yeomen of cristen blood,
That lerned in that scole yeer by yere
Swich manere doctrine as men used there,
This is to seyn, to syngen and to rede,
As smale children doon in hire childhede.

AMONG thise children was a wydwes sone,
A litel clergeon, seven yeer of age,
That day by day to scole was his wone,
And eek also, whereas he saugh thymage
Of Cristes mooder, hadde he in usage,
As hym was taught, to knele adoun and seye
His Ave Marie, as he goth by the weye.

Thus hath this wydwe hir litel sone ytaught
Oure blisful lady, Cristes mooder deere,
To worshipe ay, and he forgate it naught,
for sely child wol alday soone leere;
But ay, whan I remembre on this mateere,
Seint Nicholas stant evere in my presence,
for he so yong to Crist dide reverence.

This litel child, his litel book lernynge,
As he sat in the scole at his prymer,

CHAPTER THREE

The
ARTS and CRAFTS
TRADITION

*'The only work of art which surpasses a complete medieval book is
a complete medieval building.'*
WILLIAM MORRIS

There is no easy way to disentangle the maze of influences that surrounded book illustration at the end of the nineteenth century, for contradictions seem to abound and anomalies meet one at every turn. How was it that William Morris, the high-priest of the hand-made book, was so blind to readability and balance in his own productions? Why did leading designers working in an *art nouveau* style disclaim any connection with *art nouveau*? Why did Pennell lambast the admirers of woodcuts so trenchantly in *Modern Illustration* (1895)?[1] The answer must surely be that although the advances in reproduction, book-making and presentation gave a certain homogeneous style to the publishers of the 'Nineties, very different forces were at work beneath the surface. Foremost among these was the Arts and Crafts movement.

Where the Arts and Crafts movement is concerned, the illustration of the book was only one facet among many, the decoration, the paper, the binding, the production and the usefulness of the volume being equally important. The impetus of such men as William Morris and John Ruskin was so much towards a new order, social reform and political awareness, that it is almost impossible to think of these beautiful productions independently of architecture, the historic crafts and a proselytizing call. Some of the best work was in fact the product of guilds or societies, where craftsmen artists worked closely together. The superiority of this 'craft' element appears increasingly in the books of the 'Nineties, a vocabulary developing to foster the cause. Books are treated in this parlance as buildings and their visual ornaments as part of that architecture. With increasing regularity books are not produced but 'built'—Gleeson White refers to the new work of Ricketts as 'built on ancient models'[2]—the volumes are not 'illustrated' but 'pictured' as if by frescoes, and the title-pages bear the

'The Prioresses Tale' by William Morris (1834–96) and Sir Edward
Burne-Jones (1833–98) for *The Kelmscott Chaucer*, 1896.

names of decorators as well as artists. To crown this atmosphere of handicraft and masonry, Burne-Jones calls the Kelmscott Chaucer 'a little like
a pocket cathedral'.[3]

A flavour of this is implicit in Crane's *The Decorative Illustration of Books*
(1895): 'Now for graphic ability, originality, and variety, there can be no
doubt of the vigour of our modern black and white artists. It is the most
vital and really popular form of art at the present day, and it, far more
than painting, deals with the actual life of the people; it is, too, thoroughly
democratic in its appeal, and, associated with the newspaper and magazine,
goes everywhere — at least, as far as there are shillings and pence — and
where often no other form of art is accessible.'[4]

Crane's popularising of the arts through education, politics and reform
led him in to poster work, textiles, wall-papers, book-plates and ceramics
as well as books, the illustration of which he regarded as merely a small
part of his activity. Crane's fertile imagination produced remarkable results
in all these fields, although his socialist posters of brawny amazons and
scythe-sweeping labourers have disturbing similarities with the art of the
Fascist states in the 1930s.

This political stance tinges all Crane's later work and he seems determined to return to an ideal world of medieval myth in which a happy
commonwealth of craftsmen exists entirely to make beautiful objects.
Crane, despite his convictions, did not like depicting modern scenes. His
reputation had really been made long before the 'Nineties with his celebrated series of Routledge 'Toy Books', two or three books being produced
every year between 1865 and 1876. It was a most productive partnership
between him and the independent-minded printer, Edmund Evans, the
publishers taking a secondary role. Printed in bold, flat, three-colour wood-
engravings in the 1860s, the books became more and more complex in their
tinting and overprinting in the next ten years. They were revolutionary in
their cheapness, their simple clear statements of design and their obvious
appeal to children through the attractive shades. John Lane re-issued the
series in 1895, another sign of the nostalgia for older methods and the day
before yesterday. Most of Crane's finest achievements fall well before the
end of the century. *The House That Jack Built* (1865), *Sing a Song of Sixpence*
(1866), *This Little Pig Went to Market* (1870), *Valentine and Orson* (1874)
and *The Sleeping Beauty* (1876) all show skilled organisation of the decorative page, either conceived as a frieze or as elaborate borders in which the
text is placed. Crane also developed a penchant for incorporating music
and hand lettering into his square pages.

By the early 1880s some of Crane's books have that strong aesthetic
touch which was to be so pervasive a feature of the 'Nineties, notably in
Household Stories from the Collection of the Brothers Grimm, for Macmillan
(1882). Here his frontispiece of the 'Sleeping Beauty' is tightly packed,
gestural, romantic, but set in a Renaissance frame like the section of a
triptych. The title-page is treated like the illumination of a single initial
letter in a medieval manuscript, a contrived facade of porch and pilaster
framing diminutive figures from the story. These illustrations, set in the
pages as if they were panels or tiles in a piece of architecture, run right
through the book, as do the remarkable headpieces, colophons and decorations derived from early Italian printed books. It was precisely this mixture of the original with the pastiche that Macmillan's were using in their

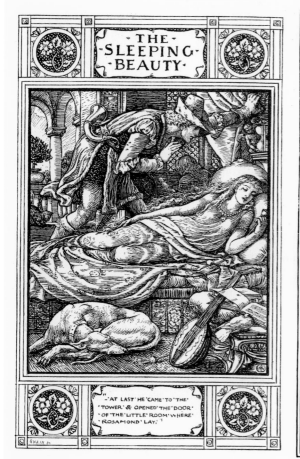
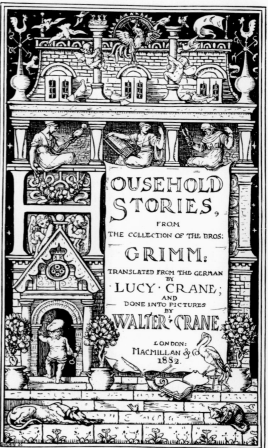

Frontispiece and title-page by Walter Crane (1845–1915) for *Household Stories* from the collection of the Bros. Grimm (Macmillan), 1882.

English Illustrated Magazine in the 1880s. A good example of Crane's work for a scholarly audience in lavish format is his page decoration for Professor George C. Warr's *Echoes of Hellas*, 1887, a sumptuous book printed in two colours on hand-made paper with a vellum binding blocked in gold. Crane decorates and illuminates rather than illustrates the pages, in a style that owes something to Flaxman; how many Victorians were classicists at heart!

Heading by Heywood Sumner for the *English Illustrated Magazine*, 1887.

The real accolade for Crane as an illustrator came in 1891, when he was invited by William Morris to contribute twenty-three illustrations to the poet's own *The Story of the Glittering Plain* (1894). Morris was so anxious to issue this production of his press that Crane's work could not be included with the first edition.[5] The wood-engraved illustrations, cut by Crane's cousins, the Leveretts, were so admired that Crane was commissioned to do another book, *Reynard the Fox*, for David Nutt in 1894. On the illustrations for *The Story of the Glittering Plain* the 'Nineties critic, Aymer Vallance, commented: 'very beautiful in themselves, but perhaps not quite free enough from the suspicion of Renaissance influence to be altogether in keeping with the Gothic character of the surrounding borders and other ornaments in whose company they are set'.[6]

The most elaborate of Crane's illustrated books of the 'Nineties was his six-volume edition of Spenser's *Faerie Queene: A Poem in Six Books with the Fragment Mutabilitie* (1897), a veritable fruit of the Arts and Crafts movement. The elaborate scheme was mooted by Allen, the publisher, as a counterpart to a successful edition of Ruskin's works and Crane worked on the designs for three years. Issued in parts between 1894 and 1896, it was edited by the bibliophile forger, Thomas J. Wise, and printed by the Chiswick Press in a limited edition of 1000 copies on hand-made paper. Crane's full-page illustrations, headpieces, tailpieces and initials are in the full blown woodcut tradition, but are somewhat heavy and stiff compared with the joyous freedom of his earlier books. It was obviously the intention of the publisher that these extraordinary volumes should invite comparison with the Kelmscott books or even with Beardsley's *Morte d'Arthur*, but they lack the technical beauty of the first or the wit of the second. The original pen drawings are rather splendid things in isolation and they demonstrate the great stature of Crane, the only Arts and Crafts artist to be given such an opportunity, although the vogue for Renaissance line was so much in fashion. Crane called it a 'congenial' task 'commenced with a light heart'.[7]

Although the foundation and work of the Kelmscott Press by William Morris falls almost exactly into the last decade of the century (it was begun in 1891 and closed in 1898), it was more influential than typical for its time. William Morris (1834–96), the apostle of good design and craftsmanship, had always been intensely interested in book production and was a student and collector of early Italian printings. He had projected an illustrated edition of *The Earthly Paradise* in 1866, but the scheme did not get beyond specimen pages. Morris then developed an interest in hand illumination, calligraphy and typography, obsessions that were to influence his work at Kelmscott, making the productions more book decoration than book illustration. In 1888 Morris attended a lecture given by Emery Walker (Editor of the *English Illustrated Magazine*) to the Arts and Crafts Exhibition Society, resulting in his having two books specially printed at the Chiswick Press with plans to design a type of his own. This led directly to the founding of his own printing house, the Kelmscott Press at 16 Upper Mall, Hammersmith. Three types emerged from Morris's design experiments, one Roman—the Golden—and two gothic—the Troy and the Chaucer.

Ornament was the starting point and Morris emphasised its importance in his essay, 'The Ideal Book'. 'The essential point to be remembered is that the ornament, whatever it is, whether picture or pattern-work, should form *part of the page*, should be a part of the whole scheme of the book.' He then went on to say, 'The picture-book is not perhaps, absolutely necessary to man's life, but it gives such endless pleasure, and is so intimately connected with the other absolutely necessary art of imaginative literature, that it must remain one of the very worthiest things towards the production of which reasonable men should strive.'[8]

Morris created his ornaments from the brush, with exemplars, incunabula and manuscripts spread out before him. This gives a certain fluidity to the designs, which one would expect from a textile and wall-paper artist, but they solidify when interpreted into wood engraving. Vallance commented on the second book from Kelmscott, *Poems by the Way* (1891), that although the borders derive from fifteenth-century Italian printings, they are more Romanesque than Gothic with their convolutions and intertwinings. Apart from Crane's contribution, these books were not heavily illustrated; Burne-Jones supplied the frontispieces to *A Dream of John Ball* and *A King's Lesson* (both 1892), and two designs to *The Golden Legend* of the same year, 'The Storye of the Byble' and 'The Legendes of Saynetes'. Neither are credited to the artist in the book.

Edward Burne-Jones (1833–98) had met Morris at Oxford in 1853, and during the 1860s and 1870s they had worked closely together in the decorative arts, notably in stained glass design and mural painting. In the 1890s they were both elderly men, so that it is surprising to find them embarking on such a project as the Press, let alone on its masterpiece, the Kelmscott *Chaucer* (1896). Both men were familiar with Chaucer's texts, having read them together at Oxford, and both studied them again for this new and sumptuous edition. The volume was in preparation for six years: the original sixty illustrations by Burne-Jones were increased to eighty-seven by 1894, and every detail of paper, printing and binding was watched lovingly by the poet-printer.

Burne-Jones was determined to stick closely to Chaucer's actual works in his illustrations, but he chose to depict the chivalric and romantic scenes, rather than the more earthy tales which would have been preferred today, and which would probably have been more acceptable to Morris too. This restraint was very typical of the artist, but it was also typical of the stamp of books in the last decade of the nineteenth century which could be daring, but superficially so. An exception to this is the beautiful illustration of a naked Venus illustrating 'The Romaunt of the Rose'. In some ways Burne-Jones' very literal rendering of Chaucer's imagery leaves little to the imagination. His illustration to 'The House of Fame' gives an impression of basket work, but the poet would have been better served by a looser and less exact reading. 'The Knyghtes Tale' which is the perfect vehicle for Burne-Jones' individual style is full of the medieval mood that he loved. The illustrations with their floating figures are reminiscent of Botticelli and also of the earlier Sienese painters, and the landscape backgrounds look to the mountains in the predella panels of Domenico Veneziano. With true Pre-Raphaelite thoroughness, Burne-Jones made detailed drawings of such things as birds and armour before incorporating them in to the narrative.

It was a mark of the changing times that Emery Walker persuaded Morris to use electrotypes instead of woodblocks to print the initial letters.

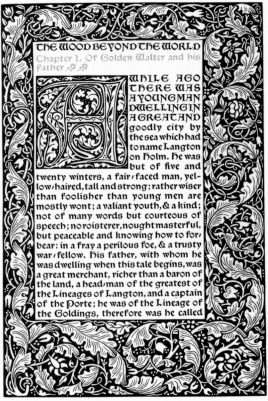

Frontispiece and title-page by Sir Edward Burne-Jones (1833–98)
for *The Wood Beyond the World* (Kelmscott Press), 1894. Wood-
engravings.

The impracticality of older methods dogged the Kelmscott *Chaucer* as it
had done the work of the earlier Pre-Raphaelite illustrators in the 'Sixties.
Burne-Jones' drawings were too fine a production to be easily interpreted
by the block-maker. Emery Walker persuaded Morris to have the designs
photographed on to a 'platino' which could be reworked by the assistant,
Catterson-Smith. Specimen pages were taken in 1893, with the text and
vine leaf borders cut on one block and Burne-Jones' illustration on a
separate one. Catterson-Smith checked any difficult passages in the blocks
with Burne-Jones himself or compared them with Dürer to see how they
were handled.

Most importantly, the Kelmscott *Chaucer* set a standard for a book to
be considered as a complete work of art. Only occasionally before this was
the page opening admired for its coherence and complimentary qualities
of type, design and paper, rather than being looked at in bits. The page
spreads of some of the poems, particularly 'The Romaunt of the Rose', are
a revelation of scale and space and were already an example to countless
students and designers before they appeared in June 1896. For Morris it
was the last statement of his ideas. He had written, 'A book ornamented
with pictures that are suitable for that book, and that book only, may
become a work of art second to none, save a fine binding duly ornamented
or a fine piece of literature'.[9]

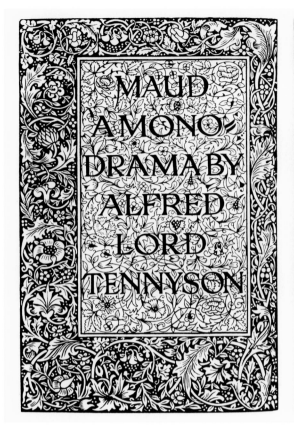
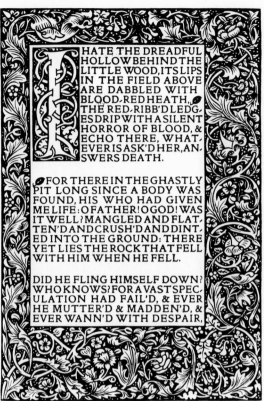

Opening pages by William Morris (1834–96) for *Maud, A Mono-drama* by Alfred Lord Tennyson (Kelmscott Press), 1893.

Widely influential as the Kelmscott books might have been, both in style and content, they were hardly typical of their era. At a time when the younger artists were trying to adapt to the new technology, Morris and his friends were being dragged reluctantly into the photo-reproductive world. Concurrently with Ricketts' brilliant attempts to lighten the page and give it greater clarification, Morris was producing exquisite frontispieces, such as that to his *Maud* of 1893, where the text of the poem was telescoped into a space to suit the design. It appeared that readability was not high among his priorities.

There was always some animosity between the Arts and Crafts devotees and the innovators like Pennell. Pennell argued that but for experiment no printer or artist would have ever got beyond the St Christopher block. 'Botticelli was looking not backward, but forward, when he illustrated the "Hypnertomachia" — if he did illustrate it. He was essentially an innovator; so was Dürer. Probably, had the illustrators Kelmscott looked up to as masters known anything about wash, had their engravers been able to reproduce it and their printers to print it, they too would have used wash, for they were no less adventurous in illustration than the makers of the American magazines. One evening, during a discussion after an Arts and Crafts meeting, Pennell was arguing in this fashion when William Morris lost his temper. "And what do you know or understand about Kelmscott

'Both the Children were sitting up' by A. J. Gaskin (1862–1928)
for Andersen's *Stories and Fairy Tales*, 1893. Pen and ink.
(BIRMINGHAM CITY ART GALLERY)
'The boy. . . . . rode into the pond' by A. J. Gaskin (1862–1928)
for Andersen's *Stories and Fairy Tales*, 1893. Pen and ink.
(BIRMINGHAM CITY ART GALLERY)

printing?" he asked. "Enough to have bought the Kelmscott *Chaucer,*" Pennell said, and that ended the argument.'[10]

The followers of Morris were really to be found in one place—the Birmingham School. It is difficult to be certain why his influence was so strong in a Midland art school; perhaps Morris's writings touched a chord in the industrial heartland, perhaps the provinces were more receptive to the seer than London. There were some close links: Edward Burne-Jones was a Birmingham man and took an interest in what went on in the city, and Morris himself had lent the Art School a complete set of the Kelmscott books for study and example. The quintessential Birmingham style is represented by one artist, Arthur Gaskin, who was popular with Arts and Crafts artists because his work so closely resembled that of Burne-Jones.

Arthur Gaskin (1862–1928) was a Birmingham man who spent the whole of his working life in the city as pupil and teacher. Gaskin was fortunate to belong to a creative group of young men who shared broadly the same outlook: Joseph Southall (1861–1944), with an architectural training and a first-hand contact with Italy, E. H. New (1871–1931), topographer, and C. M. Gere (1869–1957), book illustrator and decorative artist. In their wake was a whole band of minor illustrators who did excellent if undramatic work.

Gaskin's was probably the strongest talent illustrating alongside New and Gere in the volumes of the *English Illustrated Magazine*, 1890–93. They were regular exhibitors at the chief shop window for their movement, The Arts and Crafts Exhibition Society in London, and in 1893 Gaskin created a stir with his illustrations for *Hans Christian Andersen's Stories and Fairy Tales*. Although commercially printed, this was limited to an edition of 300 copies on hand-made paper and was very close to a private press production. Gaskin's initial letters and one hundred illustrations were cut on wood by another Birmingham talent, Bernard Sleigh. The book, with its variety of subject matter, but earnest, even-toned wood engravings of thoughtful children and reflective adults, caught the mood of Arts and Crafts society. Many of the stories are helped by the Crane trick of hand lettering, giving the tales a naive charm, and where there are decorative frames a peaceful stillness seems to come from the page, now emptied entirely of Pre-Raphaelite tension. Crane referred to them as 'full of a naive romantic feeling, and have much sense of the decorative possibilities of black and white drawing'.[11] The *Studio*, which had earlier compared the book to Crane's edition of *Grimm's Fairy Tales*,[12] went on to set Gaskin in his true context:

> Mr Gaskin has fulfilled the expectation aroused by Mr William Morris's publicly expressed commendation and proves himself a worthy recruit to those who rally round the standard of old English art, as opposed to those whose sympathies and styles are drawn from Paris, either directly or by way of America. It is a singularly satisfactory piece of book-making.[13]

Crane seems to have preferred another book Gaskin did on his own, *Good King Wenceslas* (1895), which he calls 'simple and bold, and in harmony with the subject . . .'[14] This was very much in the craft tradition, the subject commemorating a medieval ideal, the illustration and type cut into the block like a fifteenth-century block book. The *Studio* was disappointed that there were only five full-page illustrations but thought Gaskin's work 'especially excellent in its decorative rendering of stone, wood and drapery'.[15] It was equally enthusiastic over a *Book of Fairy Tales* by S. Baring-Gould, published a year earlier but reviewed in the same number. 'Henceforth Brummagem is a term of contempt no longer, but is become instead a title of honour', it proclaimed. It felt that the 'grey tone' of the *Hans Andersen* had been eliminated in the new volume and that Gaskin's design 'is arranged with well proportioned margins, so that the open page of letter press by itself, without further decoration, is a distinctly beautiful object'.[16] They felt that 'the massing of black in contrast to the lighter portions of the composition could scarcely be improved'.[17] (See page *i*)

Gaskin's mastery of traditional methods and his regard for the page recommended him to William Morris, who asked him to do two borders for Kelmscott. These were Morris's own *The Well at The World's End* and Spenser's *The Shepheardes Calendar*. Although Gaskin prepared designs for the former, Burne-Jones' work was eventually preferred. *The Shepheardes Calendar*, on the other hand, was a fine example of a Kelmscott book with something of the robustness of the *Good King Wenceslas*. Gaskin sets the figure for each time of year against a heavily patterned background of trees or flowers, but with the real 'props' of country life, the wooden hurdles and dry stone walls of his Cotswold rambles. The relationship of text to illustration and the design of the initials in this book seem happier than in many of the Kelmscott productions. Gaskin's surviving designs for *The Well at The World's End* are heavily bordered and with fewer areas of breathing white space.[18]

Gaskin's wife, Georgie Cave France (1866–1934), was a fellow student and a fellow illustrator. Her influences were also in the Arts and Crafts mould, principally Kate Greenaway, whose decorative aspects were so highly thought of, and Walter Crane. Georgie Gaskin was as versatile as her husband, undertaking Christmas cards for Marcus Ward in 1896 and designing for a series of childrens' books in that and succeeding years. This included *The History of The Hornbook* (1896) and *Hornbook Jingles* (1896–7), both published by Andrew Tuer's Leadenhall Press which specialised in books of traditional appearance. In *Calendar of the Seasons* (1897), Georgie Gaskin gives us the same ingenious childhood figures that Greenaway loved, but more 'arts and crafty' and within rather freely rendered frames. The object in this, and in the later *Little Girls and Little Boys* (1898), was to get back to the simplicity of childrens' books published by Newbery in the eighteenth century, that Tuer was writing about. Both Gaskins more or less gave up book illustrating after 1900.

Inextricably linked with the Gaskins are the names of C. M. Gere, Joseph Southall and E. H. New. Gere was a Gloucestershire man, trained at the Birmingham School of Art and launched into book illustration in 1892, when he was chosen to do the woodcut frontispiece of Kelmscott

'Kelmscott Manor' by C. M. Gere (1869–1957), frontispiece for
News From Nowhere by William Morris, 1892.

Manor House for Morris's *News From Nowhere*. Gere's work for the *English Illustrated Magazine* (1893), *Russian Fairy Tales* (1893) and *The Imitation of Christ* (1894) is not as individual as Gaskin's, but Crane said 'he thoroughly realizes the ornamental value of bold and open line drawing in association with lettering and is a careful and conscientious draughtsman and printer besides'.[19]

Joseph Southall was another Birmingham resident, closely connected with the Arts and Crafts, politics and teaching. A lifelong Quaker and pacifist, his influences came from the Italian Quattrocento, Burne-Jones and Crane. His only illustrated book was Charles Perrault's *The Story of Blue-Beard* (1895), though he did contribute to magazines. (See page *vii*)

A much more prolific artist was Edward Hort New, an Evesham man who was trained at Birmingham but is associated very much with the Cotswolds. He settled in Oxford and his books include a topographical guide to the city, *Oxford and Its Colleges* (1897). He was the very suitable illustrator of an edition of *The Compleat Angler* (1896), and *Pickwick Papers* (1897), but his métier was with buildings, old villages and such subjects as White's *Natural History of Selborne* (1900). New's pages were cleanly drawn in a rather dry, woodcut style, typical of Birmingham; he liked wide foregrounds and an absence of people. A mark of his distinction is the way he was taken up by the Bodley Head: 'Lane had a great affection for him, and he for Lane', May wrote in his biography, and New was a frequent guest at Lane's home in Albany.[20]

Distinct from the Arts and Crafts movement, though connected with it, was the etching revival which had taken place in the 1860s and 1870s under the lead of Whistler and his brother-in-law Sir Seymour Haden (1818–1910). P. G. Hamerton (1834–91) in his *Etching and Etchers*, published by Macmillan in 1875 (2nd edition, 1876), did a great deal to boost the art, which was highly popular in France. The emphasis was really on the separate plate and the printseller, rather than on the book and the publisher, although etched illustrations occasionally appeared in volumes.

Among the most important etcher-illustrators was William Strang (1859–1921) who has already been mentioned as a contributor to *The Hobbyhorse*. Recognised as an important print-maker as early as 1881, he was one of the outstanding pupils of Alphonse Legros' Slade School. Legros had a French attitude to etching as an art in its own right; he was deeply influenced by the Old Masters as well as by Millet and Courbet. It was this last element that came through so strongly into Strang's work and provided it with what Rothenstein called 'a grim and lusty inventiveness in the compositions of his subjects'.[21]

Strang's tour de force was his *Pilgrim's Progress* produced for Nimmo in 1895. Strang created this series in a rather unorthodox manner, working on the prints *before* seeking a publisher. Charles Holme, who worked for Nimmo, saw it in its early stages and called it 'the most satisfactory and desirable of the firm's publications'.[22] Strang had in fact had great difficulty in getting these etchings before the public; he told Rothenstein, 'they all wanted pretty things',[22] When one looks at this dignified, plain book, with its handsome etched title-page and clear printing, one sees why. Strang's images such as 'The Butcher and the Sheep' are bold and strong and completely uncompromising. The realism has echoes of Millet, but the timbre of Rembrandt. For a public raised on *art nouveau* it was too serious

'The Butcher and The Sheep' by William Strang (1859–1921) for
The Pilgrim's Progress (Nimmo), 1895.

a diet. The artist's distinguished career was to include other remarkable
works, single prints, measured passages from poetry and realism, all
observed with a sombre dignity. Perhaps the greatest achievement of all
was his Milton's *Paradise Lost* in 1896.

CHAPTER FOUR

AMERICAN STYLE

Although the influence of America was strengthening in the field of illustration during the 'Seventies, it probably lacked a clear spokesman until the arrival of Joseph Pennell (1860–1926). Pennell, the Pennsylvania Quaker who was lithographer, illustrator, author and teacher, had worked for all of that new breed of publications, the American magazine. He was working extensively for the *Century* (formerly *Scribner's*) and a little bit for *Harper's*, but his novelty was very much as a child of the American 'golden age' of illustration.

Pennell had been fortunate to emerge from the Pennsylvania School of Industrial Art at precisely the moment when new technology and new communication was revolutionising magazine art. *Century* magazine had a dedicated team of editors determined to use only the best authors and illustrators. This was backed up by a first-class band of engravers who were able to efface entirely their own personalities in the pursuit of artists' facsimile work. Reproductions were produced in almost perfect line and superbly printed; the superiority of the *Century* was recognised and its style infectious, so that other magazines like *Harper's* copied the ideas enthusiastically. Pennell later wrote, 'the engraver was asked to reproduce a drawing, not in the conventional manner, but as faithfully as he could, not only rendering the subject of the drawing, but suggesting its quality, the look of the medium in which it was produced.'[1] He also commended their attention to paper, stiff glazed papers, inks and the generosity of the publishers in their payment of artists. The engravers included names that became legendary: Timothy Cole, W. B. Closson, Frank French and Frederick Jungling.

Pennell came to England on a *Century* commission in January 1883, a fleeting visit en route for Venice, but giving him sufficient time to make contact with the English magazines, the *Portfolio*, *The Magazine of Art*, and the *Art Journal*. In the summer of 1884 he returned to London, this time with his new wife, the writer Elizabeth Robins Pennell, and decided to settle there; it was to be a residence that lasted with intermissions for about forty years. Although Pennell found the atmosphere of London stimulating and its closeness to the Continent a source of inspiration, he nevertheless found the British puzzling and exasperating. His forthright Quakerism endeared him to the leaders of the Arts and Crafts movement, but the dilletantes and amateurs of the art world found his trenchant views less palatable. Even so, Pennell believed passionately that the New World had something to teach the Old and set about demonstrating it.

There was already the nucleus of an American community in London. Whistler (whom the Pennells idolised) had been a Londoner for many years, but was essentially more of a Continental than an American; Sargent was not to arrive until the following year, 1885. Only E. A. Abbey, who had arrived in 1878 and was one of *Harper's* stars, could have been called established. Pennell immediately called on these artists and on Stephen Parrish, the Philadelphian who was in town with his young son, Maxfield Parrish. Within days he was going to see the master-etcher, Seymour Haden, in company with Parrish and being introduced to Ford Madox Brown and W. M. Rossetti. In the next two years the Pennells were to undertake an astonishing itinerary for their magazine proprietors in far away New York, producing 'Italy from a Tricycle', for which they pedalled from Florence to Rome, and 'Venice' for *Harper's*; they also went on a punishing tour of the English cathedrals in 1885. Pennell had hoped to join the committee of the Painter-Etchers, following Haden's enthusiasm for his work, but no Americans were elected. 'British members feared their influence and competition.'[2] There was considerable suspicion of the new-comers. After some unflattering reviews, Elizabeth Pennell commented years later, 'We began to think our nationality was our crime.' She went on, 'In the last century the Englishman's attitude to the American was one of tolerance and he was pained if the American failed to be grateful.'[3] But, despite this, the Pennells became the centre of a coterie.

It is interesting to follow the gradual awakening of interest in American artists in the late 'Eighties. The most established one of all, E. A. Abbey (1852–1911), moved in the best British artistic circles and recorded his impressions. 'Charles Green gave a studio party the other night,' he wrote at this time, 'A lot of men there. Old Dalziel was one of them, and he is most enthusiastic over the American magazines. Everybody is, but the preference is usually given to *Scribner's*.'[4]

Leafing through *Scribner's*, *Harper's* or *St Nicholas* and other periodicals, all of which were more heavily illustrated after 1890, one is aware of the rapid rise and success of photomechanical processes, notably line block, half-tone, photogravure and collotype. Editors and printers were anxious to experiment, gradually admitting grey half tones until their readers were truly familiar with process work. The early half-tones were so bland that they had to be heavily retouched by the engraver to bring out detail and contrast. Photographic process was more adaptable than engraver's work, could be enlarged or reduced easily, and was very much cheaper. These bonuses enabled the magazines to fill their pages with far more illustrations than ever before. This created what one commentator called 'a thirst for illustration', where 'the most heavily illustrated magazines seem in general to have been the most successful.'[5] It was also true that the artists whose work reproduced best under the new conditions were the ones most in demand, hence the rise of clean-cut pen drawing, chalk and wash studies, the areas that had been so difficult to interpret before. There was nothing comparable in the early 'Eighties with Pennell's ink and pencil landscapes, and from this strength of reproduction a whole school of architectural illustrators emerged.

Pennell also recorded that his own student days had been greatly invigorated by the American artists returning from Paris. The International Centennial Exhibition at Philadelphia in 1876 had been a turning point, when Americans had seen what was going on in Europe. That spring the artists Chase, Duveneck, Twatchman, McLure Hamilton and Muhrman, returning from Paris, Antwerp or Munich, were exhibiting at the Pennsylvania Academy. Pennell was impressed by the Americans' grasp of eclecticism, a grasp that he felt was lacking in Britain. William Rothenstein, reaching the French capital in the late 1880s, found much the same thing. It was the American artists that he looked to for support; the inability to speak French, and the shared pool of literature they enjoyed, seemed to bring them naturally together.[6] By the 1890s the American Arts Association there had their own periodical, the *Quartier Latin*, based on the French paper of the same name. Entitled 'A Little Book Devoted to the Arts' and published in Britain and America at 6*d.* and 10 cents respectively, it was one of the few little magazines to carry advertisements. It appeared under the Dent imprint from July 1896 to March 1899, edited by Trist Wood, and it contained a great deal of atelier chit-chat, both British and American. Its illustration was a nice mix of the two countries. The chief American contributor appeared to be Henry G. Fangel; Alfred (Garth) Jones (*fl.* 1893–1914) was doing splendid youthful work, especially a powerful 'Don Quixote' in August 1897. Other artists to make frequent appearances were: J. J. Guthrie, Oliver Onions, Philip Connard and Cyril Goldie, supplemented in later issues by Gilbert James, Jack Yeats and Dion Calthrop. The magazine published an 'In Memoriam of Gleeson White' in November 1898 and advertised Dent's books in December 1898. It boasted a colour frontispiece that Christmas but did not survive the new year.

Walter Crane was one of the comparatively few British illustrators to visit the United States, making a prolonged tour in 1891–2. Crane had been impressed by the Arts and Crafts revival there and by a guild at Boston, similar to the Century Guild in London, which produced a handsome quarterly, the *Knight Errant*, printed by the Elzevir Press, Boston with a cover by Bertram Grosvenor Goodhue. He also met W. J. Linton, his old master engraver, then residing near New York, whom he considered a beneficent influence on American illustration. But Crane was grudging about the American magazines: 'If he [Mr Pennell] will pardon my saying so, in some instances the illustrations are, or used to be, often daringly driven through the text, scattering it right and left, like the effect of a coach and four upon a flock of sheep.'[7] But his admiration for one American giant was unqualified: 'I think there can be no doubt that in Elihu Vedder we have an instance of an American artist of great imaginative powers, and undoubtedly a designer of originality and force. This is sufficiently proved from his large work — the illustrations to the "Rubaiyat of Omar Khayyam".'[8] Crane particularly admired Vedder's designs for the cover of the *Century* which showed 'taste and decorative feeling in the combination of figures with lettering'.

The *Century* was perhaps the first magazine to be published simultaneously in New York and London with comparatively similar United States and European editions. (The London version contained more articles on British artists and illustrators.) Although the line drawings were markedly superior to those of British publications in the early years, and artists such as Frederick Remington, E. W. Kemble, Arthur B. Frost and A. E. Sterner had their first European exposure, the credits to the artists were not prominent. The actual design of the magazines was on a level with the *English Illustrated*, but had greatly improved by 1896. By this time, however, there was an increasing use of photographs, much deplored by Crane.

Another important link with American publications at first hand was Gleeson White's appointment in 1890 as Associate Editor of the New York magazine, the *Art Amateur*, a low-priced rather brash production filled with line blocks and half-tones. This work gave him a great insight into how modern magazines were run and proved invaluable when he was setting up his ideas for producing the early numbers of the *Studio*.[9] Although the *Studio*'s pages were to point in the direction of Europe, it was continually aware of American art. In its first volume, 1893, it contained an important article on 'The Art Magazines of America'. This unsigned contribution, probably by Gleeson White, was flattering about their design and seriousness, but contained the following sobering reflection:

> It must suffice to say that while looking, as young England for the most part looks, to Paris as the fountain-head of modern art, they appreciate other Continental schools more fully, or at least more openly than we do, but with few exceptions pay absolutely no attention to the majority of English painters whose very names are unfamiliar to their readers.[10]

Pennell's gatherings in his house in Barton Street, Westminster brought together a good mixture of established British figures and rising Americans. Elizabeth Pennell wrote:

> The Barton Street sitting-room became a pleasant dropping-in place for friends and, as always, if his habit of speaking the truth kept the many away, it drew to him the few who understood and appreciated. Fisher Unwin, Legge, Norman, Charles Whibley, Bernard Shaw, Harold Cox, the Arthur Tomsons were some of the most constant evening visitors. And in the afternoon, at the hour of tea, the Edmund Gosses, Henry James, Austin Dobson, the Henry Harlands, the William Sharpes, Doctor Furnivall, Charles Godfrey, Leland were often with us.[11]

The English illustrators welcomed to Barton Street included Phil May, A. S. Hartrick, Raven Hill, Edgar Wilson and William Strang, often there to meet members of the *Century* staff.[12]

Of those mentioned, the most significant in this context was Henry Harland (1861–1906), the novelist and later literary editor of *The Yellow Book*. Harland had come to Europe in the same year as the Pennells, 1883, but had spent most of his time in Rome. Later visits were centred on Paris, and it was not until July 1889 that he and his wife sailed for England with a determination to settle and enjoy the 'attraction and novelty' of London. Their home in the Cromwell Road became one of the literary centres of the 1890s, but the only artist specifically mentioned by them was the ubiquitous Whistler. However, as the painter Alfred Thornton pointed

Frontispiece by E. A. Abbey (1852–1911) for *A London Garland*,
1895.

out, 'Because Harland was in revolt against the "old" fiction as we were
against the "old" painting . . . there was a certain unity for a cause'.[13]

If one had to define the essence of the new American style it would be
line. Among his contemporaries, E. A. Abbey was seen as epitomising this
sureness of penmanship and breadth of conception, not seen in England
since the 'Sixties. It was partly a distillation of ideas from France, Spain
and Germany, and it certainly showed a close study of the work of Adolph
Menzel, among others. The results were a freshness and vitality, a generous
use of the picture space, and a fine line that could still breathe on the paper
in a way that was wholly American. Two of Abbey's best productions were
published or conceived in the 'Nineties, *The Comedies of Shakespeare* (1896)
and *She Stoops to Conquer* (1901), both illustrated by drawings 'so refined
that no engraving can reproduce every line in them', as Pennell remarked.[14]

If Abbey was the most respected American artist in London, Charles
Dana Gibson (1867–1944) was the most influential. As Abbey had transformed historical illustration, so the work of the younger man was to affect
the direction of social illustration. Gibson was a *protégé* of the new magazine, *Life*, founded in 1883, and by the late 'Eighties he was being hailed
as the American du Maurier. A prodigy at sixteen, Gibson had had a little
training in New York and Paris but he possessed an innate sureness in

C. DANA GIBSON

Figure drawing by Charles Dana Gibson (1867–1944), *c.* 1895.

draughtsmanship that could not be taught. Tall, clean-cut and married to the most beautiful of the Langhorne sisters (one of whom was Lady Astor), Gibson's social credentials were impeccable. The critic, Ernest Knarff, credited Gibson with recording 'a national type' found in the places where he and his lovely wife moved; Gibson's family or relatives often recognised in the handsome men and elegant women, the Gibsons themselves.

If the background was correct, so was the marvellous ink line, and Gibson spent years refining it. As early as 1892, Gibson was in England, staying with E. A. Abbey at Morgan Hill, and again in 1896. On this occasion he came with his young wife, Irene, and hired rooms in Albany, living the fashionable life of the West End. He used his time wisely in London and Paris, capturing their social seasons and, more importantly, their social manners, on glossy white card. Gibson succeeded in creating a cast of characters in high life, based on the New York and Boston elite, but more extended than that of du Maurier. His drawings were on a very large scale for black-and-white-work, but completed with tremendous assurance and an almost poster-like use of white space and compositional sleight of hand. His album books were more like sketch-books and the observer seemed to be looking over the artist's shoulder into salons and tea parties and tête-à-têtes of great privacy. The exclusiveness of Dana Gibson's world was part of its magic, so was his creation of the proud, lovely, statuesque and well-bred being, the Gibson girl, an epitome of young America of the 'Nineties. In the eyes of many British observers, the Gibson girl was indeed synonymous with the 'Amurrican gurl', where nature was copying art. On his visit to the States in 1890, Harry Furniss of *Punch* was repeatedly asked what he thought of this ideal being; the drawings that he did of her decidedly owe something to Gibson.[15]

AT THE ROYAL ACADEMY.
Her first picture. Skied!

'At the Royal Academy' by Charles Dana Gibson (1867–1944) for
Pictures of People, 1897.

Ernest Knarff detected a change of style in the middle of the decade —
'His [Gibson's] early technique, free but overloaded with cross hatch, has
of recent years given way to a simpler style, depending for its capital effects
on outline.'[16] The same writer put this down to the influence of the simpler
lines of Forain, Steinlen and Caran d'Ache, and thought his work looked
better in volumes than in magazines.

As with Abbey's work, it was the refinement of the line that took London
by storm. As early as 1893 the *Studio* urged its readers to 'study' Gibson's
illustrations: 'the result has much of the quality hitherto deemed peculiar
to an etching'.[17] The writer might easily have been thinking of the etchings
of Paul Helleu (1859–1927) which have a certain affinity with Gibson's
penwork in stylish shorthand. Gibson was fêted in London, and became a
friend of Phil May and the du Mauriers, as well as of hostesses like Lady
Jeune. When John Lane published his *Drawings* in 1895, the reception
was ecstatic. 'On every page,' wrote the *Studio* critic, 'one sees the American
girl with her faults, her frivolities, her virtues, and her graces; and to him
who knows her as she walks her beloved Fifth Avenue or drives through
Central Park of the city of her birth, the psychological instinct as well as
the artistic talent evinced in this counterfeit presentment is nothing short
of wonderful.'[18] The *Studio* went on to make direct comparisons. 'We know
none of the younger illustrators of our own country from whose published
work could be gathered a volume of the same varied degree of excellence
as this . . .', concluding that 'to every student of illustration, and of black
and white work in particular, this beautifully and worthily made volume
will possess the very highest interest.'[19]

Gibson's crowning achievement was the one man show devoted to him
at the Fine Arts Society in 1896. Here, for the first time, in 'Drawings
Illustrating Society', the British public were able to see the actual work
rather than the reproductions, and judge his extraordinary mastery for

Illustration by Dudley Hardy (1867–1922) for *London Opinion*, 1894,
showing the influence of C.D. Gibson.

Illustration by Frank Craig (1874–1918) for *Pall Mall Magazine*,
1914.

themselves. Gibson's European labours came out in 1897 as *Pictures of People* in which such British institutions as the Royal Academy, the presentation at Court and a recruiting sergeant were featured. In his freest compositions, Gibson rises to the heights of a Helleu but some of these sketches are rather overworked as he battles with unfamiliar subjects in strange surroundings. But the impact on draughtsmanship must have been considerable. From the middle of the 1890s, a whole generation of artists grew up with the Gibson girl as their model. Older artists like Dudley Hardy (1867–1922) copied the scale and the hauteur, lesser artists such as W. D. Urquhart and W. Dewar (*fl.* 1890–1903) copied the American's work in their art schools.[20] The magazines of the 1900s and the picture pages of the novelettes were all deeply tinged with Gibsonism; the big social pictures of Frank Craig (1874–1918), though using washes and a heavy bodycolour, depicted the British equivalents of Boston or Broadway. Having fallen into this mould, Craig worked largely, though not exclusively, for American magazines such as *Harper's*.

John Lane, who was Gibson's London publisher, seized his transatlantic opportunities early. He established a branch of the John Lane Company at 140 Fifth Avenue, New York in 1896. Arnold Bennett wrote humorously, 'Oh had you not enough to do / But you must needs shock New York, too?'[21] Lane was intent on introducing a number of British writers and, more interestingly, illustrators to the American market. Married to an American and a collector of early American pictures, Lane saw no hardship in continual journeyings across the Atlantic for a business which

'Robin shooteth his Last Shaft' by Howard Pyle (1853–1911) for
Merry Adventures of Robin Hood, 1883.

he still saw as his personal concern. Lane may have made the mistake of
believing that his house could thrive on largely imported titles. At this time
the import tariff on imported books was 15 per cent levied on the British
rather than the American retail price, and although the American market
bought more books, the arrangement meant that the British publisher was
invariably the loser. John Lane's pre-eminence continued for nearly thirty
years, bringing the work of *avant-garde* artists to a new audience, but finally
the branch succumbed to financial pressures and Lane's age. 'He had
made himself a name in the literary and artistic circles of New York', his
biographer wrote, and he must have lost the connection with great regret.[22]

From Pyle's "Wonder Clock."   Copyright, 1887, by Harper & Brothers.

Illustration of 'Old Father Time' by Howard Pyle (1853–1911) for
The Wonder Clock, 1887.

Of the artists whose impact was strongest on the British scene, Howard
Pyle (1853–1911) must be ranked very highly. Pyle's pen technique was
based on a close scrutiny of Dürer woodcuts, so that his connection with
the Arts and Crafts movement was palpable and he could expect ready
admirers here. Pennell particularly commended his creative approach to
other artists, his 'way of adapting the methods of an earlier generation to
our own requirements is exactly what the old men did, and it is only by
so doing art advances. Pyle has preserved all that was good in their work,
and yet kept pace with modern technical and mechanical development'.[23]
This early style anticipates Morris and the Beardsley of the *Morte d'Arthur*.

Illustration by Howard Pyle (1853–1911) for *The Story of Sir Launcelot and His Companions*, 1907.

A second, later style was based upon the drawings of Maurice Leloir. Pennell notes in 1895 that 'he has laid aside the pen, and painted illustrations in oil',[24] an habitual practice of some book artists. Occasionally one comes across book illustrations prepared in oil on millboard (grisaille) at this date, though perhaps it was commoner in the States than in Britain. Pennell's chief criticism of Pyle's work was that his illustrations of the classics lacked a sense of locality, since he had never visited Europe.

Artists of the next generation were not neglected and a fair anount of interest was shown in the virtuoso graphic work of Will H. Bradley (1868– c. 1940). The *Studio* ran a whole article on the American artist in 1894. 'In Chicago', it claims enthusiastically, 'a decorative designer of some power and distinction, who has of late worked in the Beardsley manner, has arisen.' The writer goes on to praise Bradley as 'our modern master of the decorative grotesque'.[25] There was a clear connection with the Beardsley manner in England and the *Studio* expressed it like this:

It is not easy to state with precision at what moment in the evolution of Mr Bradley's art he came in contact with Mr Beardsley's work. The immense influence which that work exerted over him, immediately he saw it, is so obvious that the uninformed may well be excused for mistaking a Bradley of the later period for a real Beardsley.[26]

This overlooks the distinct pattern and flow of Bradley's work. His theatre poster for *The Masqueraders* certainly used Beardsley's pierrot figures stencilled with dots, but his essentially American elements were his daring use of contrasted black and whites and his dramatic page sense. His work, often richly linear and two-dimensional with borrowed stippling, has none of the brooding menace of the English artist; on the contrary, its execution is light-heartedly brash. His 'Skirt Dancer' and 'Serpentine Dancer' are very advanced for their date, the first extremely French, the

Illustration by Will H. Bradley (1868–*c*. 1940) for *The Chicago Sunday Tribune*.

'The Skirt Dancer' by Will H. Bradley (1868–c.1940).

second verging on abstraction. The eye-catching element in such works suggests a grounding in commercial art — indeed, Bradley had served his apprenticeship in advertising, a more sophisticated field in the United States than in late Victorian Britain.

Artists without Bradley's creative capacity and undoubted brilliance profited less from the bewitching Beardsley spell. C. Lewis Hind, who spent many years in America, recorded this influence in the 1900s: 'He set a fashion. Scores of lesser men imitated him, but no one came anywhere near the strength, vigour, and decision of the Beardsley line, or to his unerring decorative sense. Forgeries abound today. I was invited to an exhibition of "Beardsleys" in an American city. Joe Pennell came in, gave a hasty look and fled. "Mr Pennell doesn't like them!" said the perturbed proprietor to me. "Like them!" I cried, "He doesn't even consider them. They're too silly even to be taken seriously."'[27]

Nevertheless, at the big 'Modern Illustration' exhibition at South Kensington in 1900–1, an epilogue of the *fin de siècle*, the American representation was larger than any except the British and equal to that of Germany. It included pen drawings featured in the *Studio*'s special number, proof engravings by Timothy Cole from *Century Magazine*, and work from *Harper's* and *Life*. American illustration could truthfully be said to have come of age.[28]

CHAPTER FIVE

BEARDSLEY
and his
FOLLOWERS

'At the age when normal genius is still groping for its method, he
was the unerring master of his method.'
MAX BEERBOHM

Beardsley's is the personality that dominates the decade of the *fin de siècle*, traversing the aesthetic, moral and geographical boundaries like a colossus, but at the same time as fragile as the lotus flowers that came to symbolise the period and as enigmatic as the shadowy world they represented. Perhaps it was only in late Victorian Britain with its tradition of self-help, amateurism and hard work that such an extraordinary talent as Beardsley's could have been allowed to develop untramelled. Aubrey Vincent Beardsley (1872–98) was born in Brighton, the son of middle-class parents with an interest in the arts. He attended Brighton Grammar School where he received much encouragement, developing a taste for drawing, literature and the theatre. Beardsley had practically no artistic training other than some evening classes at the Westminster School of Art. But he did start with great advantages over many contemporary illustrators, in being first and foremost a literary animal, fluent in French, widely read in both French and English literature and a considerable prose writer.

Even in his juvenilia, done during the late 'Eighties, Beardsley displays a grasp of his subject matter, a decorative sense and a power that are seen in few adolescents. His early sketches, linked to Virgil's *Aeneid*, to Dickens, Congreve, Balzac and others, have an intensity and penetration that are highly individual; they also have a brooding, menacing satire. Beardsley's lonely childhood, shared with his sister Mabel, had all the ingredients of isolation and creativity that we associate with other Victorians like the Brontës; they included home entertainments, the writing of dramas and the development of a personal vision of the world. The young Beardsley was fortunate to have sympathetic schoolmasters, a housemaster, A. W. King, who enjoyed his drawings and a form-master, H. A. Payne, who widened his tastes.

Beardsley left school in July 1888 and went to work for a London architect, leaving in 1889 to become a clerk with the Guardian Life and Fire Insurance. In that year his chronic consumption was diagnosed, and

'How Queen Guenever rode in Maying' by Aubrey Beardsley
(1872–98) for *La Morte d'Arthur*, 1893–4, Vol. 2, Pl. 137. Pen and
ink. 8 ⅛ x 6 ⅝ ins.
(VICTORIA AND ALBERT MUSEUM)

for two years he gave up his amateur theatricals and did very little drawing.
With a remission in 1891, he began to work again and concentrated on
some illustrations for Marlowe's *Tamerlane*. This began a chain of circumstances that brought his work before the public quite rapidly. Befriended
by the bookseller, Frederick Evans, he was recommended to the young
publisher, John Dent, as a possible illustrator for Sir Thomas Malory's
Morte d'Arthur.

Beardsley and his sister visited Whistler's Peacock Room and called
on Sir Edward Burne-Jones on one of his visiting afternoons, when the
distinguished artist showed interest in his work and gave him some advice.
In the middle of 1892 he went to Paris with a letter from Burne-Jones,
called on Puvis de Chavannes, and also saw for the first time the refresh-
ingly free poster work of Toulouse-Lautrec. These contacts were new and
exciting ones for a young man whose artistic formation had been through
the works of the Pre-Raphaelites, their imitators and the picture books of
Kate Greenaway and Walter Crane. They were supplemented now by
frequent visits to the National Gallery to study Botticelli, Pollaiuolo and
Mantegna, before saturating himself in the evenings with Wagner operas.

The commission to illustrate the *Morte d'Arthur* transformed the young
artist overnight from a dilettante to a professional, but circumstances also
changed him from an unknown into a celebrity. By a happy coincidence,
a new journal of the arts, the *Studio*, was being established at precisely that
moment. C. Lewis Hind, the godfather of the *Studio*, recalled their first
meeting:

'La Femme Incomprise' by Aubrey Beardsley (1872–98), *c*. 1893. Pen and ink. Reproduced in *The Unpublished Work*, 1925.

'Le dèbris d'un poète.' by Aubrey Beardsley (1872–98) in his *Japonesque* style, *c*. 1892. Pen, indian ink and wash. 13 x 4 ⅞ ins.
(VICTORIA AND ALBERT MUSEUM)

It seems incredible, but Beardsley was then only twenty years of age; he stood behind Aymer Vallance, slim, self-possessed, a portfolio under his arm. He handed it to me. I looked through the drawings, and said to myself, 'Either I'm crazy, or this is genius.'

Here was the 'sensational send-off' that we wanted. What better than the discovery of a new genius by a new journal? I suggested that Joseph Pennell should write the articles on Aubrey Beardsley, and that Beardsley should design the cover for *The Studio*, which he did. When No 1 appeared in April 1893, it was the talk of the town in art circles.[1]

Pennell was the ideal man for the job. His measured article carried weight, he was an artist himself, and he was sympathetic to new styles and new techniques in mechanical reproduction. Pennell was impressed above all that Beardsley remained his own man despite borrowings from those he admired.

It is most interesting to note, too, that though Mr Beardsley had drawn his motives from every age, and founded his styles — for it is quite impossible to say what his style may be — on all schools, he has not been carried back into the fifteenth century, or succumbed to the limitations of Japan; he has recognised that he is living in the last decade of the nineteenth century, and he has availed himself of mechanical reproduction for the publication of his drawings, which the Japs and the Germans would have accepted with delight had they but known of it.[2]

The illustrations that are reproduced are more or less in his Japanese style, but the most significant was the double-page spread of *Morte d'Arthur* where 'Merlin Taketh the Child Arthur Into His Keeping'. Pennell calls this 'one of the most marvellous pieces of mechanical engraving' he had ever seen.

A few months later, on publication, the *Studio* devoted a further page and a half to the *Morte d'Arthur*. Of all Beardsley's books it was the most British and traditional, owing perhaps more to the Pre-Raphaelites and Morris than his other designs, but still containing the wit and power that those artists so often lacked. The *Studio* wrote of his 'balances of masses and the simplifying of forms to their most naive presentation that are so fascinating'.[3] Most contemporaries were impressed by the bold use of white upon black in these illustrations, where the design seems almost dug out of the paper. But they also noticed for the first time the 'feast of fantastic and eerie conceptions'.[4] William Morris, in particular, disliked the book; it was a direct challenge to Kelmscott and, while flattering to the great designer on the surface, had within it dangerous signs of anarchy. Ross considered that it was Beardsley's 'least satisfactory performance' but admitted that it had far more variety and invention than Morris.[5]

As might be expected, Walter Crane was not enthusiastic about Beardsley and damns him with faint praise in *The Decorative Illustration of Books*. Of the *Morte d'Arthur* he concedes that there is a 'delicate sense of line, and a bold decorative use of solid blacks' but he questions the morbidity. Crane wrote: 'There appears to be a strong medieval decorative feeling, mixed with a curious weird Japanese-like spirit of diablerie and grotesque, as of the opium-dream, about his work.'[6] The book was in any case a rival to Crane's own *Faerie Queene*, but the scent of decadence that he smelt was very close to the truth!

'How King Arthur saw the Questing Beast' by Aubrey Beardsley
(1872–98) for *La Morte d'Arthur*, 1893–4, frontispiece to Vol. 1.
Signed and dated: Aubrey Beardsley March 8 1893. Pen and ink
and wash. 14 ⅞ x 10 ⅜ ins (27.8 x 27 cm).
(VICTORIA AND ALBERT MUSEUM)

Concurrently with the large work for J. M. Dent, Beardsley was undertaking a small scale commission to illustrate *Bon-Mots* of Sydney Smith and
R. Brinsley Sheridan, edited by Walter Jerrold. Robert Ross refers to it
as 'rather silly' as a book but marvels at the artist's brilliance in decorating
it with weird grotesques. Beardsley's humour, which had revealed itself so
disconcertingly in schoolboy caricatures, needed its outlet and found it in
this little book. Although the drawings are very small they embrace everything from Japanese females, pierrots, Bosch-like images and insects to

'The Toilet of Salome' by Aubrey Beardsley (1872–98) for *Salome*
by Oscar Wilde, 1894.

disturbing foetal symbols and vignettes that seem to have originated in
some fourteenth-century monk's marginalia.

Soon after the *Morte d'Arthur* was reviewed (in 1894), Oscar Wilde's
Salome, with illustrations by Aubrey Beardsley, was noticed, revealing
quite another style. Beardsley's interest in the Japonesque had developed
side by side with his medievalism, and when the latter was discarded, the
former remained. His enthusiasm for Whistler was unbounded and he had
also had his attention drawn to the figures on the Greek vases in the British
Museum, a potently erotic source for expression and imagination. From
the Greek vase painters he assimilated the technique for showing drapery

in a few spare economically disposed lines, such as in the *Salome* frontispiece, where the bloated face of Wilde appears as the rising sun! A combination of this contrast of line and mass is found in 'The Peacock Skirt', the upper part of the picture containing the linear and the gestural from vase painting, the lower the swirling ferment of Whistler decoration. In the range of the other plates from 'The Black Cape' to 'John and Salome' and 'Enter Herodias' there are astonishing compositions, richness of concentrated detail and suggestions of colour. Crane criticised them for not being representative of pen and ink work. The *Studio* said of this book: 'Those who find it the very essence of the decadent fin de siècle will rank *Salome* as the typical volume of a period too recent to estimate its actual value and too near to judge of its ultimate influence on decorative art'.[7] Robert Ross called this set 'collectively, his masterpiece'.[8]

In 1893 the avant-garde publishers, Lawrence & Bullen, engaged Beardsley to illustrate part of *Lucian's True History* in conjunction with two very different artists, William Strang and J. B. Clark. Beardsley clearly enjoyed the work, for which he was handsomely paid, but several designs were rejected. Some of the designs are very richly patterned, others display the black and white contrast of the earlier works; another illustration, 'Dreams', is rather in the 'hair line manner' of *Morte d'Arthur*.

The year, 1894, was memorable for the founding of *The Yellow Book*. Henry Harland and Aubrey Beardsley, both tragically ill consumptives, staving off early death in feverish work, became joint editors of Lane's magazine. These two years, 1894–5, reflect changes in Beardsley's direction, but they are dealt with in the following chapter on the *fin de siècle* magazines.

Some mystery has attached itself to Beardsley's working practice, and the myth that he worked at night in a darkened room with lighted candles, is probably one that the artist himself would have enjoyed and did little to deny. It probably derived from Beerbohm's remark that nobody ever saw Beardsley at work. Robert Ross, a close friend and early biographer leaves a clear account:

> The neatness of his most elaborate designs would suggest many sketches worked over and discarded before deciding on the final form and composition. Strange to say, this was not his method. He sketched everything in pencil, at first covering the paper with apparent scrawls, constantly rubbed out and blocked in again, until the whole surface became raddled from pencil, indiarubber, and knife: over this incoherent surface he worked in Chinese white with a gold pen, often ignoring the pencil lines, afterwards carefully removed. So every drawing was invented, built up, and completed on the same sheet of paper.[9]

D. S. Macoll (1859–1949), a critic and minor painter, who had first introduced the young man to Greek vases, also recorded the line:

> He could draw with pen-and-ink lines like a spider's web, lines that most men could only attempt with the less precarious point of the etching-needle. He had the calligraphic instinct strong and firm to an extent not common in modern Western art, that is to say, it was *play* to him to show upon paper webs of spider lines.[10]

William Rothenstein, who was an acute witness to all this, corroborates Ross's and Macoll's memoirs, adding, 'He would talk and work at the same

'A Repetition of Tristan and Isolde' by Aubrey Beardsley (1872–98) for
The Savoy, 1896, No. 8. Indian ink. 7 ⅝ x 6 ⅜ ins (20.5 x 16.8 cm).
(VICTORIA AND ALBERT MUSEUM)

time; for, like all gifted people, he had exceptional powers of concentration.' He also comments on the character of the drawings and the fact
that they reflected an underlying astringency. 'But for all his craftsmanship
there was something hard and insensitive in his line, and narrow and small
in its design, which affected me unsympathetically. He, too, remarkable
boy as he was, had something harsh, too sharply defined in his nature —
like something seen under an arc-lamp.'[11] Here one has a portrait of the
'Nineties: the effortless drawings made without preliminary studies, the
concentration shrugged off with witticisms, the gold pen a natural tool of
the dandy, the imagery esoteric and fetid. In many ways Beardsley was
like one of his own creations, having a personality so sharply defined as
to be wholly unorthodox, and a mind so self-absorbed as to be nearly
amoral.

Macoll pointed out in his early appreciation that Beardsley had a great
advantage in presenting a fantasy world; there was no necessity to observe
ordinary conventions and this tipped the balance of his drama and his
satire.

If the intensity of grimace in a fantastic world gives the spectator a shock on seeing his work, this shock is heightened by the frenzied patterning of the space, the delicate embroideries and daring bars and patches of black. Such intense decorative effects exist only at one or two stages of sharply defined convention on the way to fuller naturalistic treatment. Not only is anthithesis sharper in a world of black and white and arbitrary contours, but the furniture and the creatures of this world of nowhere-in-particular are much more movable than in a world of realistic painting.[12]

In 1894, Beardsley was asked to contribute four illustrations to *The Works of Edgar Allan Poe*, published by Herbert S. Stone & Co. of Chicago. The drawings reproduced in the book were only used in the limited edition, but were re-issued in 1901. They are all bold, spacious page illustrations which show the artist as a master of contrast, the balance of black to white undeviatingly correct.

What must be regarded as Beardsley's greatest achievement came at the end of 1895 when the unscrupulous publisher, Leonard Smithers, asked the artist to illustrate an edition of Alexander Pope's *The Rape of The Lock*. It was the literary critic, Edmund Gosse, who suggested the idea, apparently aware of Beardsley's tastes and interests. Rothenstein records how Beardsley had 'explored the courts and alleys of French and English seventeenth and eighteenth-century literature' and felt at home there. The age of Pope above all gave him the chance to display the biting invective of Georgian satire with the fopperies and excesses of dress that he delighted in. As Brian Reade, author of a standard work on Beardsley, has suggested, the illustrations are far from a literal interpretation but, in the words of the title-page, they are 'embroidered' to evoke the artist's feelings for the text. In reality, the decoration expresses the sensuousness of the age of the rococo that Beardsley found so attractive; it had a lot in common with the age of *art nouveau* and was at its most effective in the use of arabesques, broken ornament and assymetry. The young artist must have had a very considerable library of engraved books to work from, and an interviewer described his 'rare copies of last century *livres à vignettes*, and various presentation copies of valuable books,' as well as 'his numerous pictures, engravings from Watteau, Lancret, Pater, Prud-'hon and so on'.[13]

Beardsley assimilated the spirit of these books without directly copying from them. Robert Ross calls him a student of Callot and Hogarth, but it is the essence rather than the substance of his great predecessors that appears in his work. The detail of Hogarth is there, but not the animation; the overturned chair of 'The Battle of the Beaux and Belles' is straight out of 'Marriage à la Mode', but *his* scene is a decorative tableau vivant. Beardsley does not set out to illustrate the text in natural terms for the poem is primarily imaginative and so the sequence of pictures are contrived stage sets; in this, too, he is like Hogarth. One critic has suggested that 'The Battle. . . .' is based on the De Guernier edition of 1714, but to my mind it suggests that Beardsley studied these earlier copies of the book.[14]

The fascination of *The Rape of The Lock* certainly begins with its binding. This is a superb example of the rococo phase of *art nouveau*, Beardsley's famed candlesticks supporting an oval which contains the offending gilded scissors of the poem. The formal design is stamped in gold on turquoise blue cloth and represents the sort of exquisite visual titillation that the reader will find within. Curiously enough, the binding of the de luxe edition with gold blocking on off-white makes a far less successful and less desirable volume. The binding is unusually signed by the artist. The cover certainly has some ambiguous forms, notably the curving borders that are supposed to represent erotic themes. This underlines the dual role of the book, that is to say a pretty volume on the surface, with profound sexual and moral inuendoes for those who look for them.

The frontispiece of 'The Dream' is in the newer style of drawing which comes to fruition in *The Rape*. Apart from the selected dark areas, the decoration is entirely formed by clever stippling, the tiny dots themselves

'The Battle of The Beaux and The Belles' by Aubrey Beardsley
(1872–98) for *The Rape of The Lock* (Smithers), 1896.

'The Three Musicians' by Aubrey Beardsley (1872–98) for *The Savoy*, 1896, No. 1.

also varying in tone and texture. An androgynous figure of a courtier peers into the heavily curtained bed, itself a sort of symbol of unrequited lust and unrelinquished virginity. The nervous prettiness of this ornamental illustration was to find itself transported in the next fifteen years into every imaginable corner of the decorative arts, from Christmas cards to the backdrops of the Ballet Russe.

After 'The Billet-Doux' illustration we have 'The Toilet' in which Belinda sits at her dressing-table, a favourite Beardsley scene, attended by her maid. The figures are costumed in a vaguely *dix-huitième* manner, although more from the 1780s than the 1700s and with the sleeves and frills of 1890s tea-gowns. Because Beardsley's skill is in the artificial enclosed world of the interior, nature does not obtrude. What appears to be a garden beyond is in reality a screen, just as, in the next illustration, 'The Baron's Prayer', what seems at first sight like a windowed landscape is actually a tapestry. One writer has stated correctly that Beardsley never depicts a landscape and even in such drawings as 'The Three Musicians'[15] the scene is a garden.

In 'The Barge' illustration for *The Rape*, the heroine is seen in the stern of a boat en route for Hampton Court, the artificiality of the setting emphasised by its ambiguity. The decoration is rich and lascivious and some commentators have picked out strongly erotic meanings in the motifs. The presence of the dwarf page, not mentioned by Pope, a symbol of immorality, is present here as he was on the dressing-table and in the succeeding plate.

The actual 'Rape of The Lock' is the most elaborate illustration in the book if not the most complex. The principal actors have changed their dress, a confusion that suggested itself to the publisher. Belinda, face obscured, as in 'The Dream' illustration, is decked out in black, the deepest colour in the whole even-toned illustration, which naturally draws our eyes to her. The Baron is costumed in the most elaborate and effeminate garb and the dwarf page-boy rifles the tea table and winks, a balance to the rifling of the lock. The curtains, garden and screen are elaborately stippled, producing a very rich effect, enhanced by Beardsley's symbolic candles. This page has close similarities to 'The Toilet' from *The Savoy* of January 1896.

The most symbolist of the drawings is 'The Cave of Spleen', principally because it shows an idea rather than an incident, and gives full scope to Beardsley's invention. By following the poem line by line one can pick out the various images mentioned such as 'Ill-nature', 'Umbriel', 'Here sighs a Jar', and 'Angels in Machines'. The picture is a dense pattern of interwoven themes as thick as a wall-hanging. The reader is encouraged to tease out their meaning, as well as to discover things not included in the text, such as the half-turned bust of Alexander Pope, itself based on the Kneller portrait.

'The Battle of the Beaux and The Belles', already mentioned, continues the decorative scheme of 'The Rape' illustration, with the principal actors in profile, and the complexity of hatching, stippling and shading, presenting an almost abstract arrangement across the page space. There are visual ambiguities in Beardsley as well as moral ones — in this case, the fall of the wigs echoed in the festoons of the curtains, and the indistinct contours of each figure giving a confused and claustraphobic atmosphere. The astonishing achievement is that although these drawings breathe the air of unreality, although they are conceived in the flat planes of his earlier work, Beardsley has invested them with a complete three-dimensionality. The last illustration, 'The New Star', completes the series as a *cul de lampe*. The book was dedicated to Edmund Gosse, its begetter, and received very subdued reviews. Was there a hidden agenda to these illustrations? Could Beardsley in a sense have been laughing at the whole of the eighteenth-century revival in book illustration? It would be typical of the artist to parody and ridicule the run-of-the-mill illustrators and to beat them at their own game. If this was the case, he happily took the themes to an excess where he created an original and brilliant style.

Leonard Smithers, who as a publisher teetered on the edge of what was permissible, asked Beardsley to illustrate an edition of *The Lysistrata of Aristophanes* in 1896. Beardsley, by now a semi-invalid, worked on the

'The Lady with the Monkey' by Aubrey Beardsley (1872–98), one
of six drawings for Gautier's romance *Mademoiselle de Maupin* (Smithers), 1898. Pen and ink and wash. 7 ⅞ x 6 ⅝ ins (19.8 x 16.9 cm).
(VICTORIA AND ALBERT MUSEUM)

designs that summer at the Spread Eagle Hotel at Epsom in Surrey. Mostly drawn in outline with no backgrounds, they derive from the Greek vase painting he had studied; they have a similar earthiness and bawdiness.

The last major change of direction came with the *Volpone* illustrations in 1898 which were unfinished at the time of his death. As for *The Rape*, Beardsley was working on them in Paris, and perhaps this contact with the architecture of the capital and its collections caused the drawings to be suffused with a richly sensuous, baroque quality. The completed initial letters were finished in pen, ink and pencil, redolent of the magisterial emblem books of the seventeenth century with their satyrs, heraldic animals and Rubensesque goddesses. Robert Ross wrote, 'For the "Volpone" drawings Beardsley again developed his style, and seeking for new effect, reverted to pure pencil work. The ornate, delicate initial letters, all he lived to finish, must be seen in the originals before their sumptuous qualities, their solemn melancholy dignity, their dexterous handling, can be appreciated'.[16]

The frontispiece was completed showing Volpone, a type of Louis XIV gloating over his treasures, as was the cover, a rich patination of flames, stamped in gold on turquoise blue cloth. This was issued in 1000 copies on art paper, the gold-stamped designs on vellum being for a special edition of one hundred copies. A related drawing, originally intended for *Volpone*, is 'The Lady with a Monkey'; this is also in the late baroque manner, the elaborate torchère on the right balancing the exotic and beribboned woman who leads a monkey on a cord. The use of pen and ink with light washes makes this series unique in the oeuvre of Beardsley; the resulting designs had to be reproduced in photogravure. Sacheverell Sitwell called it his 'Jacobean' style.[17]

After valiant struggles to survive, Aubrey Beardsley died at Menton on 25 March, 1898, with the full rites of the Roman Catholic Church. His mother had only left the sick room momentarily; when she returned, the gold pen was stuck in the floor, still quivering, having fallen from the artist's hand, It was the perfect exit for a decadent.

Beardsley's Edwardian critics glossed over the explicit sexual symbols in his work and concentrated on the quality of the drawing. D. S. Macoll says that the 'grotesque was the only alternative to insipid commonplace' in one so young, and leaves it at that. C. Lewis Hind, who understood Beardsley so little that he offered him a job on the *Pall Mall Budget* to do theatre illustrations, called him 'that youth of genius — with an evil bark and an innocuous bite'.[18] He goes on to say that his 'pictorial parleyings with what the 'Nineties called the "improper" (really quite harmless) made it talked about, gave it vogue'. The truth is that neither of these Edwardians was familiar with Freudian theories; they did not delve beneath the surface of the design into the motivations of the artist, and they were obviously not in possession of facts available to later historians. The brooding presence of predatory female figures in so many of his drawings, the disturbing incubus of the eunuch-like dwarf and the androgynous character of the chief players, speak of a very unstable sexual background. Beardsley was dominated in his life by two women, his mother and his sister, Mabel Beardsley, and in fact seldom took any major decision without them. Though he was not, apparently, homosexual, there are hints of transvestism in his letters and his relationship with Mabel was unusual, if not actually

'So she gleaned', double page by W.B. MacDougall (d. 1936), an
artist strongly influenced by Beardsley, for *The Book of Ruth*.

incestuous. The plaintive written cry from his deathbed, 'Jesus is
Our Lord and Judge Destroy all copies of Lysistrata and Bad
Drawings', was evidence enough, whatever D. S. Macoll and C. Lewis
Hind might say.

As soon as the *Studio* article of 1893 appeared, Beardsley attracted
imitators, copyists and parodists. Max Beerbohm, in his superb valedic-
tory, referred to the hue and cry of the succeeding years:

> The 'Beardsley boom' as it was called, had begun with *The Yellow Book*,
> and it had ceased with the *Savoy*, and Beardsley had, to all intents and
> purposes been forgotten by the general public. For more than a year,
> he had been living in this or that quiet place to which invalids are
> sent. There were no new 'Beardsley posters' on the London hoardings.
> The paragraphists of the London Press gradually let him be. His
> book of fifty collected drawings created no outcry, for even the book
> reviewers could no longer assert that he did not know how to draw,
> and the tattlers at tea-parties had said all they had to say about him
> long ago, and had found other objects for discussion. But while it
> lasted, how fierce the 'Beardsley boom' had been.[19]

The Beardsley boom spawned imitators in America and imitators on the
Continent. As we have seen, some of the American artists such as Will
Bradley and Frank Hazenpflug, adopted the style with wit, panache and

'Summer' by John Thirtle (*fl.* 1896–1902), an entry in the *Studio* Prize Competition, 1896, showing the effect of Beardsley in the art schools.

without plagiarism. In Germany, too, there was an intelligent response. The distinguished satirical magazine, *Fliegende Blatter*, the German *Punch*, had developed a tradition of able draughtsmanship, but the two new Munich magazines, *Jugend* and *Simplicissmus*, created a whole group of vigorous black-and-white artists who learnt much from the Beardsley School. Foremost among these was Thomas Theodor Heine (1867–1948), a founder of *Simplicissmus* and a noted Beardsley admirer, whose work for the magazine, *Pan*, has strong influences from *Morte d'Arthur*. Eric Preetorius (b. 1883) was a theatre designer from Munich whose posters have strong Beardsley overtones, and Marcus Michael Douglas Behmer (b. 1879) was drawing grotesques for *Simplicissmus* in 1900 that reflect the Beardsley manner. Slightly later, one finds Leon Bakst (1866–1924) adapting costume design from a Beardsley synthesis in his ballet 'The Sleeping Princess' and Paul Klee (1879–1940) epitomising the whole attitude of the Jugendstil in his satirical etchings of 1904–5. A German illustrator who captures the decorative end of Beardsley's work is Julius Diez (b. 1870) who illustrates *Der Liebersbrief*. Writing in 1900, Dr Hans W. Singer said of Diez and Beardsley, 'There is this similarity between them, to be sure, that they prefer to draw strange things rather than draw things strangely'.[20] Diez's intense stippling, contrasts of black and white and brooding mystery, form a link between the decadence of the 'Nineties and the Ballet Russe decadence of Bakst and Kay Nielsen.

The fact that the style of the *fin de siècle* seems so much more coherent in Germany than in Britain, must have much to do with the unifying presence of these magazines. Both *Jugend* and *Simplicissmus* were wholeheartedly associated with the new art in a way that *Punch* or *Black and White* never were. *The Yellow Book* and *The Savoy* were important for advertising the work of Beardsley and the younger school, but they were comparatively short-lived. There was nothing comparable in this country to the sumptuous *Pan* of Meier-Graefe, Berlin, 1895–1900 or the Vienna Secession periodical *Ver Sacrum*, 1898–1903, but both these publications recognised that the movement was more decorative than illustrative in content. The Paris Exhibition of 1900 provided an important crucible, where these continental influences were assimilated by British artists and the Beardsley manner was more widely seen in Europe.

Aubrey Beardsley cast a long shadow into the Edwardian book and beyond. There were artists such as Mabel Dearmer (1872–1915) who copied his mannerisms for children's books, and Léon Solon (1872–1957) who adapted figures and motifs for ceramics; Ilbery Lynch (*fl.* 1905–25) produced some witty pastiches and James Hearn, signing himself 'Wierdsley Daubery', some less funny ones. Sidney H. Sime (1867–1941) was one of the few followers able to invest his drawings with a real sense of menace and the supernatural, but he was essentially an original artist who merely used Beardsley ideas to express his own macabre world.

Two later illustrators who inherited something from the tradition of *Salome* and *The Rape* were Austin Osman Spare (1888–1956) and Alan Elsden Odle (*fl*.1921–48). Spare developed from the mystical side in the 'Nineties, Odle from the more literary tradition and, in particular, from Beardsley's flirtation with the eighteenth century. A closer successor than either of these is to be found in the weird book illustration and powerful Celtic stained glass of Harry Clarke (1891–1931) but this is well out of our chosen period.

Most of Aubrey Beardsley's contemporaries appreciated that his vision, like his technique, was too individual to copy. Many of them searched for sources for his inspiration, particularly in the work of Félicien Rops, but this was strenuously denied by his friends. An art that was both extremely eclectic and extremely personal defied slavish imitation. Robert Ross wrote that 'what he took he endowed with a fantastic and fascinating originality', adding, 'Imagination is the great pirate of art, and with Beardsley becomes a pretext for invention'.[21]

Forgeries abounded, but Max Beerbohm understood how little stature they had beside an original:

> Beardsley's *Yellow Book* manner was bound to allure incompetent draughtsman. It *looked* so simple and so easy — a few blots and random curves, and there you are. Needless to say the results were appalling. But Beardsley was always, in many ways, developing and modifying his method, and so was always ahead of his apish retinue. His imitators never got so far as to attempt his later manner of his *Rape of the Lock*, for to do that would have required more patience and more knowledge of sheer drawing than they could possibly afford. Such a design as the 'Coiffing' which came in a late number of the *Savoy*, and which has often seemed to me the most exquisite thing Beardsley ever did, offered them no possible short cut to talent.[22]

CHAPTER SIX

THE YELLOW BOOK
and the
MAGAZINES

*'Despite all criticism then and now the Yellow Book did mark a
new era in England and shook the older generation out of its complacency
by enabling it to see in the concentrated form of a single volume the
new trend in art and letters. . . .'*
ALFRED THORNTON

The one name that is totally synonymous with the 1890s is John
Lane's *The Yellow Book*, which needs to be dealt with on its
own as both a microcosm of the *fin de siècle* and an important
trendsetter. Like other memorable publications, everyone claimed to have
had a hand in its foundation. D. S. Macoll had suggested a periodical
containing art and literature; the American, Henry Harland, claimed that
he had hatched it with Aubrey Beardsley, and Arthur Waugh claimed to
be in at its birth at the National Club, Whitehall on 3 January, 1894! The
fact is that there was a need for such a publication, and the contributors
were all to be found in that close-knit circle that surrounded its publisher
and instigator, John Lane.

J. Lewis May, who wrote the life of the publisher, sets the scene and
explains why Lane was crucial as contact and catalyst:

> Beardsley and John Lane were—we see it now—a natural and inevi-
> table combination. All this is not only because Lane was Lane: it is
> no less because Lane dwelt in Vigo Street, King of a tiny, highly
> favoured little Kingdom bounded on the east by Nash's Regent Street,
> and more especially the old Café Royal, and on the west by the
> Hogarth Club. Northwards, it extended perhaps as far as the Café
> Verrey and southwards, scarcely farther than Piccadilly. A special
> light illumined that miniature realm, in comparison with which all the
> surrounding tracts were drab and crepuscular, so crepuscular that
> even Mr William Heinemann, who yielded nothing in brains or enter-
> prise or energy to John Lane, shone with less, or at least with a
> different effulgence.[1]

Prospectus by Aubrey Beardsley (1872–98) for *The Yellow Book*,
Vol. 1, April 1894. Signed with the artist's emblem. Indian ink. 9 ½
x 6 ⅛ ins. From the collection of John Lane.
(VICTORIA AND ALBERT MUSEUM)

The Yellow Book

An Illustrated Quarterly

Volume I   April 1894

London : Elkin Mathews
          & John Lane
Boston : Copeland &
          Day

Title-page by Aubrey Beardsley (1872–98) for *The Yellow Book*,
Vol. 1, April 1894.

The cafés and the brasseries that were growing in the 'Eighties, flowered in the 'Nineties and were the unofficial board rooms of the new magazines. Each clique had its favourite haunt: Arthur Waugh was to be found at 'Gourmets', or 'Petit-Riche', Charles Holmes with E. V. Lucas at 'Roche's', others at 'Evans' Silver Grill'. Holmes remembered this intimacy at 'Roche's': 'The small tables were for couples and family parties; the round table was left to those who, like Max Beerbohm, might wish to be apart with friends; the long table was the *rendezvous* for the rest of us, so much so that the presence of any stranger, particularly near the head of it, was felt to be an intrusion.'

Some of the restaurateurs were patrons of the artists and illustrators. Degas, who had a suspicion of commercial galleries, advised Rothenstein,

'Show in colour shops, in restaurants — anywhere but at the brothels that picture shows are.'[2]

All the artists met at the Café Royal, where Oscar Wilde held court, and the contributors to *The Yellow Book* were to be found. 'Wilde's corner was like a combined outer office of the Bodley Head and the *Fortnightly* and *Saturday Review*; indeed, it was a literary bureau in itself.'[3] The main meeting place was the Domino room, an exuberant interior of mirrors, plasterwork and caryatid figures, more Second Empire than Decadent and strangely at variance with the artists who dined beneath them.

Remembered as the textbook of decadence, *The Yellow Book* was intended to be no such thing. Lane, who was later to emerge as a very cautious figure, was anxious to have a broadly based periodical, a view emphasised by Arthur Waugh who said that the new publication would deal not with 'the passing moment and its interests, but (in so far as it deals in criticism at all) with the permanent and the stable'. William Rothenstein, on the other hand, recalled the admixture of new and old. 'Meanwhile, Lane feverishly reaped the harvest of decadence', Rothenstein wrote, 'He started *The Yellow Book*, the first number of which included most of the names now associated with the 'Nineties. Oscar Wilde, Aubrey Beardsley, William Watson, John Davidson, Crackanthorpe, Lionel Johnson and Lord de Tabley were Lane's strong men.'[4] The first two were destined to make the magazine both famous and infamous, by association and contribution; the others were intended to redress the balance. Nevertheless, *The Yellow Book* came to be regarded as the trumpet call of decadence and Beardsley's particular province. 'He *was* *The Yellow Book*,' C. Lewis Hind remembered, 'He designed a different skittish cover for each number, front and back, and four times a year we all turned the pages of the new *Yellow Book* for the Beardsleys; and when there was no Beardsley, as sometimes happened when he was too ill, how blank that issue was!'[5] This became the accepted view, but it does not diminish the stature of Beardsley to say that the magazine was a vigorous and diverse arts publication and widely influential.

Before the appearance of the less well known *Century Guild Hobby Horse*, there had been no magazines run on similar lines or with such a high quality of production. *The Yellow Book* was not just a clarion call to the aesthetes; it was bound like a serious book, its advertising was confined to modest publisher's pages at the end, and its paper and type were well above average. The pages were set in Caslon old-face type and the volumes were designed rather than merely printed, with wide margins, clear headings and fly titles before each illustration. With the literary editor, Henry Harland, aged thirty-three and the art editor, Aubrey Beardsley, aged twenty-one, it was very much the magazine of the moment and of the *jeunesse dorée*. Its cloth covers in resplendent yellow were startling; they certainly earned Lewis May's description of Lane's window display, 'creating such a mighty glow of yellow at the far end of Vigo Street that one might have been forgiven for imagining for a moment that some awful portent had happened, and that the sun had risen in the West'.[6]

Both front and back covers, scrupulously designed by Beardsley, effected a carefully poised equilibrium of format to lettering. The title-pages, by the same artist, were at first sight effortlessly simple, but in fact they contained complex relationships, of black to white and of line to type, with

'L'Education Sentimentale' by Aubrey Beardsley (1872–98) for *The Yellow Book*, Vol. 1, April 1894.

a strong dose of oriental verticality. All this was perfectly adapted to process reproduction.

The first volume of April 1894 certainly included many of the names of the new art, R. Anning Bell, Walter Sickert, Will Rothenstein and Laurence Housman, but for safety's sake there were also two studies by the President of the Royal Academy, Sir Frederick Leighton. Another feature that set *The Yellow Book* very much apart was its qualitative use of these drawings as illustrations. They were listed as 'Pictures' and they do not illustrate texts at all. If this was not a statement of Art for Art's Sake then nothing was.

From the early spring of 1894 Beardsley's striking posters, of assymetrical design, consisting of a panel showing a statuesque woman printed in blue on yellow paper, and advertising *The Yellow Book*, were to be seen at booksellers. This, combined with the Beardsley design of the prospectus, then circulating, depicting a darkly clad, gaunt female searching through a tray of books by lamplight, gave a distinctly liberated tone to the new work. Why was she choosing her own reading matter? Why was she out after dark? An equally ambiguous presence was the lighted figure of the bookseller dressed as pierrot in the doorway, said to be a portrait of Lane's partner, Elkin Matthews.

This in itself had the seeds of dire consequences, for Matthews was not invited to the grand launch of *The Yellow Book*, starting a rift which eventually led to the dissolution of the partnership. The publication was celebrated by a dinner on 16 April, 1894, at the Hotel d'Italie in Old Compton Street, an event attended by many of the artists and contributors. The guests included George Moore, John Oliver Hobbes and W. B. Yeats; notable among the artists was Walter Sickert, Joseph Pennell being represented by his wife. Arthur Waugh recalled a witty speech by Sickert who looked forward to the day when authors would be compelled to write stories and poems around pictures, hardly appropriate for *The Yellow Book* but already happening in some areas.[7] That such a remark could be made at all shows the heights that illustrative art had attained in this gilded decade.

The effect of *The Yellow Book* on the critics was extraordinary: *The Times* called it 'a combination of English rowdyism and French lubricity';[8] the *Spectator* attacked with more pointed venom: 'Be mystic, be weird, be precious, be advanced, be without value', it hissed. The new periodical had achieved a *succès de scandale* which was not exactly the notoriety that Lane had intended. Henry Harland went to France to enlist the support of P. G. Hamerton, a critic of the older generation, whose feelings were printed in an essay in the second volume of July 1894. Dealing separately with the literature and the pictures, Hamerton wrote of the design:

> The yellow colour adopted is glaring, and from the aesthetic point of view not so good as a quiet mixed tint might have been; however, it gives a title to the publication and associates so perfectly with the title that it has a sufficient *raison d'être*, whilst it constrasts most effectively with black. Though white is lighter than any yellow, it has not the same active and stimulating quality.[8]

Hamerton then launched into an appraisal of Beardsley's work which was far from uncritical and which Lane had hoped would allay the fears of more sensitive readers:

> There seems to be a peculiar tendency in Mr Beardsley's mind to the representation of types without intellect and without morals. Some of the most dreadful faces in all art are to be found in the illustrations (full of exquisite ornamental invention) to Mr Oscar Wilde's 'Salome'. We have two unpleasant ones here in 'l'Education Sentimentale'. There is distinctly a sort of corruption in Mr Beardsley's art so far as its human element is concerned, but not at all in its artistic qualities, which show the perfection of discipline, of self-control, and of thoughtful deliberation at the very moment of invention. Certainly he is a man of genius, and perhaps, as he is still very young, we may hope that when he has expressed his present mood completely, he may turn his thoughts into another channel and see a better side of human life.

Hamerton had picked out at once that contradiction in Beardsley, the exquisite decorative sense and 'his extreme economy of means', and the chilling or evil quality of the subject matter. Hamerton pinpoints the Beardsley mannerisms which today would be regarded as the symbols of the new art: 'a persistent tendency to elongation', 'a habit. . . . of making faces small and head-dresses enormous'. But he returns again to the paradox of Beardsley: 'The rarity of beauty in his faces seems in contradiction

'The Reflected Faun' by Laurence Housman (1865–1959) for *The Yellow Book*, Vol. 1, April 1894.

with his exquisite sense of beauty in curving lines, and the singular grace as well as rich invention of his ornaments.'[9]

Plaudits, though not much space, are given to Joseph Pennell for his 'Le Puy en Velay' and a similar space to Walter Sickert's two drawings. These atmospheric studies are not really illustration; Hamerton defines them as 'painter's pen work' which 'does not show any special mastery of pen and ink'. The critic is also less than fair to one of the most lovely things in the volume, Laurence Housman's 'The Reflected Faun' which he calls 'founded on early wood engravings' and describes as 'drawn with the same hardness' throughout. As a matter of fact the intensity of the line is relieved by areas of white and there is sufficient air within the picture space to make the image breathe. The only other illustration to gain a mention is Anning Bell's contribution of a pretty but modest book-plate.

'Comedy-Ballet of Marionettes' II, by Aubrey Beardsley (1872–98)
for *The Yellow Book*, Vol. 2, July 1894.

The second volume, to which Hamerton contributed his essay, was as well balanced as the first, the cover and title-page being vintage Beardsley, and the title-page having the brilliant organisation of black to white that gives the artist's work a near abstract construction. The art editor groups his six drawings together, a wise move in a magazine whose weakness could have been a lack of continuity. These include the strangely disturbing 'The Comedy-Ballet of Marionettes' (in two sections) with its preoccupied female figures and its explanatory dwarf or dwarfs who cynically address the viewer. The 'Garçons de Café' must be one of the finest Beardsley images, owing a debt, surely, to the Parisian work of Félix Vallotton. 'The Slippers of Cinderella' are in an altogether different style of white on black, and the 'Madame Réjane' is in silhouette approximating to the 'Mrs Patrick Campbell' of the earlier volume.

'Garçons de Café' by Aubrey Beardsley (1872–98) for *The Yellow Book*, Vol. 2, July 1894.

This July 1894 number is likewise strengthened by Philip Wilson Steer's sparkling portrait studies (the first wittily ambiguous), two lovely ink and chalk drawings by E. J. Sullivan and contributions by Walter and Bernard Sickert. A. S. Hartrick's 'The Lamplighter' is more typical of magazine illustration of the day, Aymer Vallance's playing card designs more typical of *art nouveau*. W. B. MacDougall is a strange artist to find here, his 'Idyll' a brooding subject quite unlike his normal book ornament and uneven displays of black and white. It is quite clear that the art editor eschewed the appearance of any other strong black-and-white artists, although his supremacy made such a policy meaningless.

Volume III carries this practice further: Beardsley has three acknowledged works and two pseudonymous ones; Sickert and Steer appear once again, and only William Hyde is there with an unrepresentative landscape. Max Beerbohm has a marvellous caricature of George IV that prefaces his own essay on the monarch and looks unaccountably like Wilde.

The grouped Beardsleys include three masterpieces: 'Portrait of Himself', moving into the wholy decorative phase; 'The Wagnerites', a black scene with the lights in reserve or painted on with chinese white, and the

'Portrait of Himself' by Aubrey Beardsley (1872–98) for *The Yellow Book*, Vol. 3, October 1894.
'La Dame aux Camélias' by Aubrey Beardsley (1872–98) for *The Yellow Book*, Vol. 3, October 1894.

'La Dame aux Camelias' which seems to point ahead to Poiret and a host of fashion designers. Beardsley's own sexual repressions and feelings of inferiority come through these dominating female presences; on the cover, as well as inside and on the title-page, the androgynous harlequinade reflects his duality.

Good things can be found in Volume IV, January 1895. Beardsley contributes a powerful front cover of a disdainful woman being offered a flower by an epicene youth, a clever disposition of black-and-white, and a delightful tall title-page of a woman's be-ribboned back. At the rear of the book (seemingly a chosen place for the artist) we have 'The Mysterious Rose Garden', a strangely beautiful symbolist plate, the sinister 'Repentance of Mrs. . . . .' and the precise and actualistic 'Portrait of Miss Winifred Emery'. At the close of the book was his frieze-like 'Frontispiece for Juvenal', where monkeys carry a sedan chair through a Regency scene, a plate borrowed from Leonard Smithers.

The other contributors include Sickert, Conder and Wilson Steer in their painterly book style, Only the mysterious Patten Wilson with his complex black-and-white illustration of 'Rustem Firing the First Shot'

'The Wagnerites' by Aubrey Beardsley (1872–98) for *The Yellow
Book*, Vol. 3, October 1894.

represents the authentic pictured page of the 'Nineties. William Rothenstein contributes a portrait of John Davidson, one of the series of so-
called 'Bodley Heads', but Miss Sumner, with her landscape, seems rather
out of place in such company.

Before Volume V could appear in April, 1895, disaster had struck John
Lane's fragile little Vigo Street world. On 5 April that year, Oscar Wilde's
libel suit against Lord Queensberry collapsed, and on the same day Wilde
was arrested at the Cadogan Hotel. Lane felt that Beardsley's art was so
associated with the Wilde circle that it would be risky to have him still
featured in *The Yellow Book*. It was a poor judgement, for Beardsley had
never been close to Wilde and the dismissal was to cost the publication
dearly. Beardsley was fired as art editor, his current work for the April
issue cancelled, and only a spine and back cover by the artist were retained,
perhaps in error. Harland, who was in Paris, had nothing to do with the
expulsion and fully expected Beardsley to appear once more in the July
issue.

'The Mysterious Rose Garden' by Aubrey Beardsley (1872–98) for
The Yellow Book, Vol. 4, January 1895.

'Rustem and the Simoorg' by Patten Wilson (1868–1928) for the
Studio, Special Winter Number, 1900–1.

To link Wilde with a major illustrator was a great mistake; there was no such association in the public mind. The painter and writer, Graham Robertson, left this profound comment on Wilde and the fine arts: 'He was not often to be found in studios, for, despite his attitude as the Apostle of Art, he did not really either care for or understand pictures, a fact that painters very quickly found out. He could and did talk bravely of them before the laity, but before artists he was perforce silent — and he did not like to be silent.'[10]

Volume V was a very poor thing. It contained drawings by Wilson Steer, Walter Sickert and Alfred Thornton, and a fine ink by the up-and-coming illustrator, Patten Wilson, once again. Volume VI was better and contained two strong images by William Strang, an idyll by A. S. Hartrick, as well as a fine Conder, 'Souvenir de Paris', and two more Wilsons. These last, 'A Penelope' and 'Sohaab Taking Leave of his Mother', are splendid story-book pieces in crisp black-and-white and the only things within the covers that pass muster as real 'Nineties work. The literary content remained surprisingly good, with stories or essays by Henry James, Arnold Bennett and Kenneth Grahame.

With Volume IX, John Lane's Bodley Head again attempted to recoup some of its earlier strengths by going to a school for contributors. This happy choice fell on the Birmingham School (which we have already considered) whose members were strong in illustration and, consequently, this is one of the most homogeneous numbers since the departure of Beardsley. For April, 1896, we have the stark, dry, but decorative 'Fishing Home' and an equally typical townscape by E. H. New. Mary J. Newill contributes a moonlight study of trees, white on a dark background, and Florence M. Rutland, 'The Lady of Shalott' in a grainy, woodcut style so associated with Arts and Crafts. There is the inevitable work by the Gaskins, a Rossetti-ish Gere painting and two pictures from ballad land: E. G. Treglown's 'Three Blind Mice' and Evelyn Holden's 'Binnorie O Binnorie'.

For July 1896, and Volume X, the choice ought to have been as success-ful but it was not. The selection of another School, Glasgow, found it in one of its most interesting phases of development, but the strengths were in decorative art, architecture and textiles rather than in book art. We are too early for Jessie M. King and not late enough to see the Macdonald sisters at their most representative. The book begins with a strong, swirling, Celtic title-page but leads on to the painterly approach of Mrs Stanhope Forbes, J. H. McNair and Charles Conder. The most typical are Nellie Syrett's 'The Five Sweet Symphonies' and the pen drawings of D. Y. Cameron.

The effect of Beardsley's departure from *The Yellow Book* was the establish-ment of *The Savoy*, whose first number appeared in January, 1896, as a direct rival, with Arthur Symons as editor. This was started by the unscrupulous Leonard Smithers, an out and out plagiarist and forger, not unacquainted with pornography, who nevertheless recognised and ben-efited from Beardsley's genius. Beardsley's own galloping tuberculosis, and

'The Abbé' by Aubrey Beardsley (1872–98) for 'Under The Hill'
for *The Savoy*, No. 1, January 1896.

his changes of mood from frenzied activity to hopeless debility, had their
outworkings in these illustrations. The artist was specially receptive to
sexual fantasy at this period and the designs for *The Savoy* prospectus and
first illustrations were withdrawn by the watchful Smithers.

The Savoy was a more complete publication than its predecessor had
been, and Beardsley was able to illustrate his own texts and consequently
to enjoy greater freedom. The cover of No. 1, a titanic woman and a
cavorting putto in an arcadian landscape, is quieter than for the other
magazine, and has black printing on pink boards. Within are many of the
Bodley Head names: Max Beerbohm, Conder, Will Rothenstein and C. H.

'The Toilet' by Aubrey Beardsley (1872–98) for 'Under The Hill'
for *The Savoy*, No. 1, January 1896.

Shannon, but there are more French artists and more Beardsleys, eleven
counting the title-page and cover. (See page *ii*)

All the Beardsleys belong to his last rococo phase where his love of the
eighteenth century is taken to new heights of exuberance, the most notable
feature of the handling being the exquisite hatching and delicate dotting
in 'The Three Musicians' or the mannered tapestry-like textures of 'The
Abbé' and 'The Toilet'. These certainly compare with *The Rape of The Lock*
illustrations, and the third drawing, 'The Fruit Bearers', for *Under The Hill*,
a projected novelette by the artist himself, has an almost Renaissance
richness in its mannered decoration and frieze-like treatment. Beardsley's

loosely inserted Christmas card is rather prosaic; perhaps the suggestion of the editor, it demonstrates Beardsley's inability to supply subjects on demand.

The second *Savoy*, of April 1896, carries a defiant statement by Arthur Symons: 'I wish to thank the critics of the press for the flattering reception which they have given No 1. That reception has been none the less flattering because it has been for the most part unfavourable.' As well as the Beardsley cover and title, there is his masterly 'Rape' and three plates at the back of the book: 'A Footnote', the haunting 'Ascension of Saint Rose of Linn' and the sinister 'For the Third Tableau of Das Rheingold'. Elsewhere in the magazine are macabre visions by that strange artist, W. T. Horton, a caricature of Beardsley by Max and a sketch by A. E. Sterner.

In the third volume we have a sad postscript by Symons which was to spell out the future of *The Savoy* and Smithers' hopes: 'In consequence of Mr Beardsley's severe and continued illness, we have been compelled to discontinue the publication of "Under The Hill" . . .' From this time forward, Beardsley's work was to be spasmodic and often from material that was readily available rather than specially designed for the number. The July cover of figures in a formalised and terraced rose-garden was, like his title-page, vintage Beardsley. The only other major contribution by the artist was 'The Coiffing' on page 100, a delicate pattern of line and stipple with restricted shading to accompany his poem 'The Ballad of a Barber'. Elsewhere there were four watercolours or engravings by Blake and an archetypal caricature of Arthur Roberts by Max Beerbohm.

The Volume 4 of August 1896 has a Beardsley cover and a repeated title-page, but nothing else by the ailing artist. That is not to say that it is without interest, for there is a delightful French scene by Joseph Pennell, a lithograph by T. R. Way and two further W. T. Hortons. The most interesting performer is Charles Conder with his fanciful frontispiece to Balzac, borrowed from the publisher. The literary contributors remained extremely impressive with poems from W. B. Yeats and Ernest Dowson and essays by Ford Madox Hueffer.

The Watteauesque cover for the September issue is one of Beardsley's best. Two strange, brooding, self-contained women stand by a heavily umbrageous lake while a satyr's mask leers from an ornament. Beardsley's love of ambiguity makes him sign with a false signature. The number was padded out with more Blakes, a pen-and-ink by the French artist, A. K. Womrath, and a good black-and-white piece by Mrs Dearmer. The strangest Beardsley work here is 'A Woman in White', a sketch in white on toned paper (not necessarily anything to do with Wilkie Collins' novel).

Both the October and the November *Savoys* are very mixed. Both have Beardsley covers and titles, and two major Beardsley illustrations. In the first we have the 'Death of Pierrot', showing a striking use of line, tone and stipple to suggest costume and character, one of the finest things to appear in these pages. The fixation with fate and pessimism is reflected in the second illustration of 'Ave Atque Vale', an exquisite play of black and white, most daring in its application of dark hair and dark trees as well as in the oddly balanced compostion. Surprisingly, Volume 6 has a jolly Phil May sketch, perhaps to offset the sombre mood of Beardsley, and to a lesser extent of W. B. MacDougall and W. T. Horton. Volume 7 has a free Celtic design by *The Yellow Book* contributor, Fred Hyland, as well as another Womrath and Dearmer. Yeats, Dowson and Havelock Ellis combine to enliven the literary side.

The last *Savoy*, of December 1896, is the most remarkable, for it is entirely the work of the two editors, Arthur Symons and Aubrey Beardsley. It contains in all fourteen illustrations by Beardsley, ranging from big pages to tiny vignettes. They include the very ambivalent 'Mrs Pinchwife' from Wycherley's *The Country Wife*, the night subject of 'A Repetition of Tristan and Isolde' and the Watteauesque 'Don Juan Sganarelle and the Beggar'. 'Frontispiece to *The Comedy of the Rheingold*' is perhaps influenced by Parisian poster art, while the 'Alberich' is the most disturbing and unpleasant image in the volume. In all these preoccupied, aloof figures, there is the energy as well as the unhealthy pallor of the consumptive.

Symons' epilogue was a rather bitter complaint, not just against Victorian values, but against the whole of society. 'The action of Messrs Smith & Son,' he wrote,

> in refusing to place 'The Savoy' on their bookstalls, on account of the reproduction of a drawing by Blake, was another misfortune. And then, worst of all, we assumed that there were very many people in the world who really cared for art, and really for art's sake. The more I consider it, the more I realise that this is not the case. Comparatively very few people care for art at all, and most of them care for it because they mistake it for something else . . . art cannot appeal to the multitude.[11]

It was the old cry of the aesthete against the philistine. But it was only half the story. The fashion for the decadent and the shocking was beginning to wane, and though its death throes were protracted for another half dozen years, a more robust art was starting to emerge. The circulation of *The Savoy* must have been fairly small, even judged by the standard of *The Yellow Book*; it is now a very much rarer item, seldom found in complete runs.

Of the legion small magazines which flourished in the middle 'Nineties, the *Butterfly* is much the most attractive. Like all the others, it was the brainchild of just a few artists who remained its stalwart and sole contributors. In this case Leonard Raven Hill (1867–1942) and A. Golsworthy produced 'A Humorous & Artistic Periodical Published on the 15th of each Month, Price 6*d*.' in May 1893. It was printed 'For the Proprietors', who were these same young men, and according to an early source the illustrations were done free! It was a tall octavo, the shape and the style giving the impression of a sketch-book, and it was superbly designed. The main contributors beside the editors were Maurice Greiffenhagen and Oscar Eckhardt, with some literary *feuilletons* by John Gray. The illustrations are particularly French and posterish even in the small scale, and rely more than other magazines on the half-tone page. But what captures the imagination is the work of Edgar Wilson, a marvellous decorative artist whose head and tailpieces (aptly named because they are often of fish) reveal an unending power of invention in a broadly Japanese idiom. The Continental bias is increased by occasional character studies by the French artist and London resident A. Besnard (1849–1934). Raven Hill reveals himself to be amazingly versatile and his pen and chalk work show a great diversity of style. For some reason the *Butterfly* expired in February 1894; perhaps the announcement of the impending *Yellow Book* was too much for it.

Headpiece for the *Butterfly*, Vol. 1, 1899 by Edgar Wilson (d. 1918).

Another series began in March 1899 under the imprint of Grant Richards and with Raven Hill in a principal role. In volume form it is an ordinary octavo in white cloth with a handsome gold-stamped *art nouveau* device on the cover, perhaps by Wilson.

In Volume 1, Raven Hill's work is still dominant, but there are plenty of beguiling decorations and initial letters by Edgar Wilson, playing on the butterfly theme, borrowing outrageously from the Japanese repertoire, or, in a couple of instances (pages 18 and 38), mischievously plagiarising the *Dial*. Wilson's soft pencil drawings in half-tone extend this range in remarkable pages such as 'Silenus', the figurehead of a ship, or in Whistlerish glimpses of the Thames, 'Under Lambeth Bridge'. S. H. Sime alternately amuses and horrifies in 'On Desperate Seas' and 'The Cabman of Harley Street' in which a ghoulish hansom is driven by Death. Raven Hill's broad spectrum of work takes in animal studies, a wash drawing of pigs, vigorous figure comedies in the Keene tradition which are much like his *Punch* work, and a most remarkable pen drawing of a 'Centaur attacked by a Bull' which could well be by Shannon. Greiffenhagen's frontispiece, 'The Princess Lands', is a brilliant piece of patterning which the critic James Thorpe calls 'delightfully decorative and colourful',[12] despite its being in half-tone and with the colour confined to shading. The elegant figure on the left may well be intended as a portrait of Ricketts.

There is a greatly extended pool of talent in Volume 2: sinister work by S. H. Sime, *dix-huitième* contributions from D. C. Calthrop, and very French black-and-white work by J. W. T. Manuel. Pennell contributes and so does Max Beerbohm, with a wickedly funny caricature of the Prince of Wales, 'The Royal Box'.

'On Desperate Seas' by S. H. Sime (1867–1941) for the *Butterfly*, Vol. 1, 1899.

'Monte Carlo' by J. W. T. Manuel (d. 1899) for the *Butterfly*,
Vol. 1, 1899.

The *Butterfly* expired for the second time in 1900, the victim of its
own high standards. It remained non-commercial and unequivocally in the
hands of its dynamic artist editor. James Thorpe summed it up very well:
'No magazine, in England at any rate, has contained in a short life of
twenty-two months such a wonderful collection of fine black-and-white
work. From this point of view it is undoubtedly the most artistic periodical
publication we have ever had, fully representative of the best work of the
nineties, and its failure is a reflection on the deplorable lack of intelligence
and appreciation in this country.'[13]

Modestly priced at 1*s*. (compared with 5*s* for *The Yellow Book*) was the *Dome*, 'a Quarterly containing Examples of All the Arts'. This slim volume first appeared on Lady Day, 1897, and was probably directed towards students and art lovers of slender means. It contained more on architecture than its rivals and had a section devoted to music in most numbers. H. W. Brewer drew cityscapes and Paul Woodroffe embellished the musical scores, but the tone is not especially *fin de siècle*. The second number had a four-block coloured wood-engraving by William Nicholson of 'The Fisher'.

The third *Dome* is more avant-garde, containing a delightful Laurence Housman of 'The Well in the World' and work by Alan Wright, Dion Calthrop and J. J. Guthrie. The progressive phase was continued in the issue for New Year's Day, 1898, with a fine Celtic woodcut-style composition, 'Wotan's Abschied', by Alan Wright and a charming 'Cranford' School picture by Malcolm Patterson. At this point the magazine goes into a new series in cloth covers, and Volume 1 contains excellent etchings by William Strang, two powerful coloured woodcut portraits by Gordon Craig, probably borrowed from his own publication, and a Lucien Pissarro. An interesting curiosity are the illustrations and accompanying text on Althea Gyles from the pen of W. B. Yeats, entitled 'A Symbolic Artist And The Coming of Symbolic Art': 'I indeed believe that I see in them a beginning of what may become a new manner in the arts of the modern world.' Althea Gyles (1868–1949) is one of those artists who have almost sunk without trace. She was very much part of the Celtic Revival and this is why Yeats lauds her so strongly. She is recorded as a poet and designer of books, a friend of Symons and Dowson, who became in 1899 the mistress of Leonard Smithers. She later illustrated *The Harlot's House* by Oscar Wilde, published by J. W. Luce, Boston in 1910.[14]

Volume 2 for January to March, 1899, has a mixture of literary contributions from C. J. Holmes, Laurence Binyon and Roger Fry, and a number of symbolist illustrations by G. Moreau. The most notable works are the splendid portrait drawing of Stephen Phillips by Will Rothenstein and a charming bibulous woodcut of 'Dumas Papa' by Gordon Craig. The next volume combines a good Housman, 'Cauchemar', a fine Strang, and an interesting three pages of illustrated poems, the text inset among the pictures of the ubiquitous Alan Wright. Volume 4 for August to October, 1899, is more lively still, with a series of early woodcuts by the Birmingham artist, Bernard Sleigh (b. 1872), some very Gaskinish, architectural plates by Will Mein, H. W. Brewer and A. Hugh Fisher, and uncharacteristic, almost Jugendstil landscapes by W. T. Horton. Towards the end of the book there are grouped works by Charles Pears, Bernard Sleigh and Philip Connard, and a very *art nouveau* poem by G. M. Ellwood.

By 1900 the art content is largely but not wholly of old masters, a scholarly text by C. J. Holmes accompanying them. Contemporary illustration is represented by three lithographs by the Dundee artist, Stewart Carmichael (b. 1867), and a borrowed illustration from a book by F. O'Neill Gallagher. There is a 'New Year' drawing by Percy Bulcock and items from Sleigh and Mein. All in all, the *Dome* is something of an *hors d'oeuvre*, lacking a strong decorative sense.

Student publications certainly made the most interesting visual books among the lesser magazines, especially if they have that homogeneity sug-

'Vintage' by Robert Burns (1869–1941) for the *Evergreen*, Autumn
1895.

gested by belonging to a particular art school or city. One of the best was
the *New Evergreen* which appeared in 1894 and described itself in its altered
state, The *Evergreen*, in 1895 as 'A Northern Seasonal Published In The
Lawnmarket of Edinburgh by Patrick Geddes And Colleagues . . .' It was
also published by T. Fisher Unwin in London, but its flavour was distinctly
Scottish, and its connection with the famous educationalist, Patrick Geddes
(1854–1932), gave it added weight north of the Border. The erstwhile

editor, W. B. MacDougall, felt so confident of its status that he sent an inscribed copy to Beardsley! It received adverse criticism from the start, most wittily from H. G. Wells: 'Bad from cover to cover and even the covers are bad.'

From the beginning there is a strong Celtic influence with pronounced initial letters and a certain high seriousness of tone. Most of the young artists are associated with Scottish teaching, some with the Old Art School, Edinburgh and a few with Glasgow. The magazine is too early for Jessie M. King and Annie French, so we have to be content with lesser luminaries such as Robert Burns, John Duncan, the head of the School, and J. Cadenhead. The first two are the principal illustrators and they display a mastery of black-and-white contrast that it would be difficult to equal in the south — this is particularly true of Burns' 'Natura Natures'. In Autumn 1895 they are joined by E. A. Hornel with a vigorous painting, and in Winter 1896–7 there is a marvellous piece by Burns, 'Aslargon's Knight', where the artist places house, lance and landscape in the picture space with the geometry of a Uccello. A. G. Sinclair provides a softer expression

'Madame Chrysanthème' by E. A. Hornel (1864–1933) for the *Evergreen*, Autumn 1895.

of black-and-white with his 'Winter Harvest'. There is no doubt that this coterie of illustrators was influenced by Japanese woodblock print in a more mature way than were most others. More subtly than their fellows they seem to grasp the spaces, the planes and the way objects need not be treated with total realism. Writing forty years afterwards, still too close to the time, James Thorpe calls it 'dour'and 'Scotch' and finds it altogether less interesting than we do.[15]

Another major student production was the *Quest*, published by Cornish Brothers of Birmingham, and printed on the presses of the Birmingham Guild of Handicraft. Beginning in 1894, its cover of black designs on grey paper and the hand-made paper inside, mark it out as a distinctly Morris-influenced product. Some of the artists are discussed in the chapter on the Arts and Crafts, but it is important to deal with this paper with the magazines. The main designs were carried out by a few Birmingham artists — Harry A. Payne, Ernest Treglown and E. H. New — the younger students being given rather peripheral jobs of decoration. Treglown's first frontispiece, 'The Quest of the Soul's Desire', is the real stuff of Kelmscott and Harry A. Payne's 'Fine Flowers in Old Valley' presents script within decorative borders in a way that Crane would have approved.

In March 1895 Payne is joined by Gere, and together they illustrate 'Warkworth', but a tailpiece is provided by the up-and-coming Violet M. Holden. E. H. New draws one of his craft landscapes of old world streets for the July 1895 number and Sidney Meteyard contributes a 'Defence of Guenevere' in the late romantic style. In November, the Guild features the well-known illustration of Kelmscott House by C. M. Gere, originally engraved for *News From Nowhere* with the block lent by William Morris himself. This number had some very good work in it, with pages that get away from the very dry, grey picture-making of many of the School. These include 'Dream City' by Louis Davis, a fine fanciful thing, and a full-page illustration by Mary J. Newill of children in a large leafed glade as well as 'The Story of Tobit' but the work of Gere, Treglown, Meteyard and Payne together is perhaps out of proportion.

The later numbers do not quite keep up this momentum. In March, 1896 that remarkable figure, Joseph Southall, has a full-page drawing, 'The King's Quair', and in July, 1896, E. H. New features 'Warwick' in one of his careful, shadeless views and G. T. Tarling provides a full-page in his best Morrisy manner. Like so many brave projects, the magazine did not last very long; its sixth issue was its final one.

The *Quarto*, though less consciously arty than all these magazines, was fairly substantial. Published by J. S. Virtue & Company, it was in essence a shop window for the Slade students and their associates. Its preface refers to the burgeoning artistic periodicals of the time: 'The appearance of a new periodical has, in these days, become a matter of such common occurence as hardly to require any introductory comments. It is interesting to notice that every new venture of the kind is started with the idea of supplying a long-felt want. Herein lies the sole peculiarity of "The Quarto": we cater for none, our aim is to produce a good artistic volume . . .'[16] The title-page, with its vignette by Nellie Syrett and narrow, vertically arranged lettering, is striking if not new. The preface heading by Cyril Goldie (1872–1942) is a highly decorative arrangement in thick black borders, carefully defined, but flowing. A good proportion of the work is by established

'The Legend of St Cuthbert' by Robert Spence (b. 1870) for the
Quarto, 1896.

figures such as Alphonse Legros, George Clausen, Fred Brown and Joseph
Pennell, but the works most markedly in *fin de siècle* idioms are by the
younger generation. Outstanding is the crowded drawing with Millais
overtones, 'The Legend of St Cuthbert', by Robert Spence (b. 1870), a
remarkable figure artist; there is a 'Nativity' by Paul Woodroffe and 'Feeding Time' by Alice B. Woodward. Her drawings are free as well as humorous: she has something of the imaginative sweep of Charles Robinson but
she is also clearly influenced by the Orient, and the Dutch School of
illustrators. A book-plate by another woman artist, Dora Curtis, seems to
have been influenced by Robinson's *Garden of Verses*, although the line is
almost Glaswegian. A great surprise is Ambrose McEvoy illustrating a
ballad in pen and ink.

The following volume (also dated 1896) keeps up the standard. As well as excellent drawings — scarcely illustrations — by the stalwarts Henry Tonks, Joseph Pennell and Jacomb Hood, there are lovely things by younger artists. Woodroffe designs a whole clutch of initial letters and also the decorative endpapers, and Nellie Syrett, a powerful evocation of 'Prince's Progress'. But Cyril Goldie's 'The Brink', of a brooding, malevolent witch seated in a symbolist landscape, steals the show. Goldie is a relatively unknown figure who etched and worked in watercolour as well as in black-and-white. He was steeped in classical landscape and the old masters and images from both spheres recur in his work. Alfred Jones (1872–*c*.1930, also known as Garth Jones) produced 'Der Erlkonig', the most vigorous and masculine illustration in the book.

In 1897 Paul Woodroffe becomes more prominent in the *Quarto*, designing the title-page — a complex pattern of Celtic scrolls intertwining flowers — the endpapers and initials. There is a strong representation of Pre-

'Feeding Time' by Alice B. Woodward (1862–1911) for the *Quarto*, 1896.

NELLIE
SYRETT.

Illustration by Nellie Syrett for the *Quarto*, 1896.

Raphaelites in these pages, but Robert Spence's 'The Legend of Fra Angelico' carries their tradition forward into a grainy bit of late romanticism. A. Briscoe with his 'Allegory', and Rosie M. Pitman with 'Undine', present attractive drawings in a late Pre-Raphaelite style that is even-toned, if derivative. Like its predecessors, the issue carries musical scores and, in this instance, good literary contributions from G. K. Chesterton and A. E. Housman.

The last of the series, the volume for 1898, has an excellent small classic work by Laurence Housman, 'Antaeus', a memorable chalk character study, 'Philip Clissett', by Maxwell Balfour and numerous bold decorations from Alfred Jones. 'March' by Miss E. Buckton is very much a Birmingham School landscape and A. Briscoe's 'The Peacock Dress' is a particularly good example of Beardsley's influence on the art schools, the patterning of black and white being feverishly copied without any of the original artist's vigour and intellect. Nellie Syrett repeats her formula of

'The Brink' by Cyril Goldie (1872–1942) for the *Quarto*, 1896.

finely drawn, if static, medievalism and F. C. Dickinson has a hard and sinister fairy illustration. There is a strong element of the 'Sixties throughout, perhaps influenced by Ricketts and Shannon, whose double lithographic portrait by Will Rothenstein is found here, together with articles by Gleeson White.

The two volumes of the *Pageant*, 1896 and 1897, edited by C. H. Shannon and Gleeson White, are really gift-books, but because they came out in succeeding years they may be included among the magazines. According to Rothenstein, the project was the brainchild of Ricketts and Shannon together: 'Ricketts was to design the cover and to look after the lay-out; and besides all the great swells, several of us younger men, Conder, Max Beerbohm and myself, were to contribute.'[16] Rothenstein persuaded Whistler to send a lithograph and Verlaine a poem. With a title-page designed by Selwyn Image and endpapers by Lucien Pissarro, it embraced all good design from the days of the *Century Guild Hobby Horse* to the time of the private presses. The beautiful initials must have been designed by Ricketts, and there is more work by his circle — Savage, Conder and Rothenstein — than by anyone else. The 1897 volume is uniform and has less avant-garde illustration than the first. It was originally provided with a striking outer wrapper (we would say dust-jacket) designed by Gleeson White. There are many contributions by Ricketts and Shannon's French heroes, Gustave Moreau and Puvis de Chavannes, as well as the black-and-white work of Savage and Housman, but perhaps best of all is Lucien Pissarro's sparkling colour woodcut in five blocks, 'The Queen of The Fishes'.

Small magazines abounded in the 'Nineties but few survived for more than a few months. Mention should be made of the *Beam*, edited by Alfred Jones, which was the organ of the students of the National Art Training School. It appeared bi-monthly in 1896 and its greatest strengths were in its editor's work and a single appearance of Housman, as well as a rare contribution by Oliver Onions, later author and critic. The *Acorn*, produced at the Caradoc Press from 1905–6, is too late for our period, but it retains some of the *fin de siècle* preciosity and has frontispieces by Frank Brangwyn.

The *Idler*, edited by Jerome K. Jerome and Robert Barr from early 1892, was not an art magazine, but at various times it gave opprtunities to the illustrators of the 'Nineties, and in later years ran excellent articles on them. In the first volume, the editors introduce the work of Dudley Hardy (1865–1922) whom we shall deal with in a later chapter. Hardy's Dutch and Parisian training make him a breath of fresh air in the grey pages of story illustrating. Hardy was in Paris only a few years after Rothenstein,

'The Peacock Dress' by A. Briscoe (b. 1873) for the *Quarto*, 1898.

Illustration by J. Bernard Partridge (1861–1945) for *Voces Populi*,
1890.

making contact with such figures as Léandre, Steinlen and Willette.[17] The
magazine also enlisted support from J. Bernard Partridge (1861–1945)
who had joined the staff of *Punch* the year before and contributed humorous
pages about artists. Partridge was an amateur actor and some of his best
works are theatrical studies of this date, beautifully conceived figure drawings, the roundness and texture built up by very careful shading. His great
success had been his *Punch* illustrations of F. Anstey's *Voces Populi* (1890),
which had appeared in book form from Longman's the same year. The
work was a series of playlets, almost extended captions to *Punch* jokes, and
ideal for Partridge's stage-struck talents, the gesturing, grimacing figures
fitting perfectly into the pages. His billiards illustration to *Voces Populi* is
rather Continental and very suave. After 1901, Partridge was to be used
increasingly by *Punch* for political work, so that this lightness of touch is
forgotten. J. F. Sullivan provides the *Idler* with joky, petit-bourgeois subjects in the manner of Weedon Grossmith's *Diary of a Nobody*, and in the
middle 'Nineties there are title-pages by Hal Hurst, posterish illustrations
by Max Cooper, and youthful efforts by T. H. Robinson.

CHAPTER SEVEN

The
BROADSHEET
and
POSTER STYLE

'. . . wood engraving, being a difficult task, lends the hand precision,
perhaps some style, is a tough craft, and one to grow fond of.'
E. GORDON CRAIG

The Victorians' self-satisfaction about their inventiveness and their progress was anathema to some of their contemporaries. We have seen how alien it was to William Morris and how distasteful to the romantics who followed the tradition of Rossetti. There was, however, a third group of illustrators who sought for a return to the old methods allied to modern expression, and who wished to capture the popular art of the past while remaining firmly in the late nineteenth century; their method was the woodcut and their medium, the broadsheet and the poster.

The mid-Victorians had developed a great taste for antiquarianism in book design. Imitations of medieval bindings, illumination and black letter abounded, but nothing quite like the revival of the broadsheet had appeared before Joseph Crawhall's Newcastle printings. Joseph Crawhall (1821–96), the son of a prosperous burgher and rope-maker from Newcastle-upon-Tyne, was an amateur artist, antiquary and sportsman. The fact that he was a Northumbrian was of considerable significance, because it was in Newcastle that the Bewick School of wood-engravers had flourished and where their productions were still highly prized. In Crawhall's youth, Thomas Bewick's pupils were still at work and he was familiar with the chapbooks of the journeyman printers like W. Davison of Alnwick, whose tiny ballad volumes had something forceful and earthy about them. A more tangible link was provided when Crawhall became the executor of Bewick's aged daughter.

As a collector of old books, an enthusiast for country lore and a man of means, Crawhall was ideally placed to indulge his fantasies. This took the form of designing and printing his first book in 1859, *The Compleatest Angling Booke*, which embodied all his enthusiasms, piscatory and typographical, and included some delightfully crude woodcuts which he cut for his own amusement. Only forty copies of this unique book were printed, and as his two brothers contributed it was very much a family venture.

Crawhall's humour and individuality come out strongly in his woodcuts, giving personality and punch, sadly missing in much Victorian illustrated literature. It may have been this unique quality that encouraged him to pursue his idiosyncratic talent, although still for a limited audience. *Ye loving ballad of Lorde Bateman To itte's owne Tune herin sette fforth*, 1860, was the next publication, with the Crawhall arms hand-coloured, and in 1864, *A Collection of Right Merrie Garlands for North Country Anglers*, hand-coloured with some compilations from the first book. There were to be nineteen of these books by Joseph Crawhall, each containing the individual imprints of its unusual author and illustrator. By the 1880s, Crawhall's excesses were more in line with public taste for the ancient and the quaint, and his work attracted the notice of Andrew Tuer of the Leadenhall Press. From 1884, he and Crawhall issued books on a more commercial basis, and reached a much wider public. These books included *Old Aunt Elspa's ABC* and *Old Aunt Elspa's Spelling Bee*, both based on the children's books of a hundred years earlier. Tuer extended the range of Crawhall's talent by producing advertisements for Brooke Bond Tea and Pears Soap, a rare combination of Victorian advertising and humour.

Crawhall's work was a conscious bid to remove the impersonal from the nineteenth-century book and endow it with vitality once again. He was both decorator and illustrator, so the crudeness of the cuts and the variability of the hand colouring gave it an 'expressionist' quality. Effectively simple, Crawhall used stippling for his backgrounds, often with a symbolic figure standing out from a black area in the manner of early books. He also liked to cut away the background to emphasise a bold black outline, a mannerism which was to be extensively copied. The coarse paper and the yellowing of age give some of these books a very antique appearance.

C. S. Felver has written, 'Crawhall had apparently already [1859] developed a sensitivity for the wood and its special possibilities as a graphic medium, possibilities that were overlooked to a large extent by Bewick, the Dalziels, Swain, LePere, indeed almost all of the great nineteenth-century wood-engravers, who seemed trapped by the concept that wood was the best medium for reproducing water-colour sketches and drawings.'[1]

It would be a mistake to think of Crawhall as an isolated and provincial eccentric. He was a scholarly collector of rare books and a close friend of the *Punch* artist, Charles Keene (1823–91). In some of the later books Crawhall's brilliantly talented son, Joseph Crawhall Junior (1861–1913) and his friend, the artist J. J. Guthrie, contributed animal and figure subjects. Good examples are in *The Compleatest Angling Booke* (2nd edition, 1881), and in *Olde ffrendes wyth newe Faces* (1881). The younger Crawhall's precocious talent and ultimate success as an animal painter in an impressionist style are probably due in large measure to this encouragement.

The wider distribution organised by Tuer gave Crawhall a certain notoriety, and his amusing antiquarianism was admired and imitated by a few specialist artists and publishers. The influence took some time to percolate through, because it was not until nearly ten years after the first issue of Crawhall's book *Olde Tayles Newlye Related* (1883), that more serious artists began to take notice. In about 1893, the Crawhall books were suddenly discovered by the younger artists Edward Gordon Craig, William Nicholson and James Pryde, the last two celebrated for the poster designs they produced as the Beggarstaff Brothers. Craig recalled that Nicholson

'Ye three leghorns' by Joseph Crawhall Junior (1861–1913). Pen
and ink. *c.* 1890.
(PRIVATE COLLECTION)

was particularly fired by Crawhall's work, 'which he loved immensely —
and those started him going'.[2]

Edward Gordon Craig (1872–1966) was the multi-talented son of the
Victorian actress, Ellen Terry, and her architect lover, E. W. Godwin. He
had had a colourful and varied upbringing, with a strong emphasis on a
stage career. But his latent interest in the visual arts was inspired by
woodcut work in the early 'Nineties, and he struggled painstakingly to
master the craft. He contacted a wood-engraver's supplier, Lacy Evans of
Red Lion Court, Fleet Street, and purchased some re-surfaced boxwood
blocks and tools with which to experiment. William Nicholson encouraged
him, suggesting that he use a photograph in which highlight and shadow
were deeply contrasted, trace it on to a woodblock and simply cut out the
highlights. Craig attempted this with a photograph of Walt Whitman and
the result was very successful. Craig wrote simply in his memoirs: 'I never
went to any art school, so I never learnt to draw — nor how to paint — and
this is why I cannot paint or draw now. William Nicholson and Stephen
Haweis — these two showed me, the first how to hold a wood-engraving
tool and a block of wood and how to cut on this with that and not cut
one's hand by slipping.'[3]

Craig continued to learn the method while working on tour as an actor,
but his career as an illustrator would not have developed if he had not
suffered disappointments in acting and stage-designing. His frustrated

115

'The House' by E. Gordon Craig (1872–1966) for the *Page*, 1898.
Woodcut.

ambitions in simplifying the stage are reflected in his experiments with woodcuts. '. . . being actor trained, I could only do my bit on a public stage — a curtain had to rise at a certain hour on a certain date, to rouse me. This curtain rising was the first number of *The Page*. Only a few copies were printed, and fewer were sold. I worked hard at its creation — many woodcuts, slight text. It appeared from 1898 to 1901 — it cost next to nothing — only life.'[4] In this modest way, Craig describes his little magazine containing his own woodcuts and a few contributions from friends. The idea was that it should augment his small income from designing book-plates.

In early 1898, the *Page* appeared on the tables of artistic people, a sombre cover of coarse brown wrapping paper with woodcuts, literary snippets and book-plates inside. The editor stated at the close of the magazine that 'The illustrations are original and are designed and cut in our offices . . . Each month we shall publish two book-plates, one already in use, one looking for a master'. Rothenstein described the *Page* as 'a magazine of which, so far as I could see, he [Craig] was the sole editor and art editor, and all the contributors and illustrators himself'.[5]

The essence of the *Page* was its dash and impetuosity. On one occasion Max Beerbohm and Rothenstein drew caricatures of each other and, on the spur of the moment, these were included. On another occasion, Craig urged Rothenstein to contribute 'Some easy considered bit'.[6] Craig's attitude to his little magazine, and indeed to his woodcuts, was somewhat ambivalent. He referred to his woodblock of Ellen Terry published in the *Artist* of June 1898 as 'worthless as a work of art'. In 1899 he wrote, 'This year I cut eighty-seven of my designs on boxwood blocks — most of them poor stuff'.[7] But of course it was not poor stuff; the cuts were an exciting and vital aspect of the artistic life of the 1890s which in other aspects was languishing into trite *art nouveau* formuli. Craig produced seventy-two woodcuts in 1898 and eighty-seven in 1899, the high point of his engraving career.[8]

The individuality which Craig could inject into his productions is nowhere more striking than in the second volume of the *Page* for 1899. The editor included his own 'Waiting for the Marchioness', 'D'Artagnan's Man' and a brilliant, tiny endpiece of a teapot and a beaker. In addition, there were hand-coloured supplements: 'The Incorruptible', an eighteenth-century subject, and 'Miss Mary Sheppy', as well as the famous book-plates

'The Lacquey' by E. Gordon Craig (1872–1966) for the *Page*, 1899.
Woodcut.

which included one for Carl Michaelis of a poodle on wheels. Craig had contributions from Conder, J. J. Guthrie, Rothenstein, Woodroffe and Pryde, but his own unique stamp was always apparent. The *Page* was metamorphosed from a monthly to a quarterly and was now sold yearly at 10*s.* in an edition of 400 copies. Various combinations of subjects were to come out in the following years including two book-plate books, a pot pourri of *Page* illustrations and the *Page* Edition de Luxe. In the last volume of the *Page*, 1901, Craig pays tribute to his mentor with an article entitled 'Some Thoughts Suggested by the Art of Joseph Crawhall'.

The *Page* also advertised Craig's *Book of Penny Toys*, or more correctly, *Gordon Craig's Book of Penny Toys*, the first title having been usurped by another illustrator, Mrs Dearmer. With his interest in simple craft and design, Craig had been collecting wooden toys sold by passing gypsies or obtained from traditional sources in Holland and Germany. Twenty

'The Trumpeter' by E. Gordon Craig (1872–1966) for the *Venture*, 1903.

'Girl Reading' by The Beggarstaff Brothers (J. Pryde and William
Nicholson), reproduced in the *Poster*, 1895.

designs were made from these in chunky woodcut style, each preceded by
a verse and the whole printed with bold type on thick buff-coloured sugar
paper. All the illustrations were coloured by hand, and Craig and volunteer
friends set about the task of preparing fifty copies for the binder. With its
ample format and its sparkling areas of colour, the book remains one of
the most desirable of 'Nineties hand-made publications.

Even after the demise of the *Page*, Craig continued to draw for illustration, much of this work reflecting the looser eighteenth-century style of
his friend, Charles Conder. As late as 1903, he was contributing stark
woodcuts to the *Venture*, and he was to go on in 1908 to create the theatrical
magazine, the *Mask*

The Beggarstaff Brothers, William Nicholson (1872–1949) and James
Pryde (1866–1941),were closely associated with Craig at this time; their
styles were similar, they admired the same artists, and in 1893 they were
living close to each other in country cottages in Buckinghamshire. The
brothers-in-law (Nicholson was married to James's sister, Mabel Pryde)

were concentrating on the new art of the poster, freeing it from the clutter of commercialism and giving it a distinctly British identity. They developed a severely simple manner, which was based on cut out work and collage rather than brush, and looked initially to France for its inspiration. Even artists like Dudley Hardy, who had trained in Paris, crowded the poster space with colour and letterpress. By contrast, the Beggarstaffs presented striking images which proved more influential than commercially viable.

Such posters as 'Girl Reading' (1899) reduced the figure to areas of colour, the last outlines only emerging where they struck background tints or where the eye intuitively said they should. The artists also cleverly inserted dark vertical features like railings or pikes to divide the picture space, tricks absorbed from Japanese art and Renaissance paintings. They exhibited at the International Pictorial Poster Exhibition at the Aquarium and produced work for the theatre, magazines and chocolate manufacturers. Much that was learnt here was transported into the important series of picture books issued at the end of the 'Nineties.

The partnership had really broken up before the books appeared between 1898 and 1900, so that Nicholson's achievement is his alone. All his books were done for the publisher, William Heinemann, Whistler's friend, with whom Nicholson had a good working relationship and for whom he designed the firm's windmill colophon. Heinemann's advertisement with the image of a merry chapman set the scene for what the volumes were meant to represent. The volumes were square quartos, printed in a slightly archaic style with large black bordered illustrations and comparatively little text: *An Alphabet*, *An Almanac of Twelve Sports* and *London Types* (all in 1898), *The Square Book of Animals* (1899) and *Characters of Romance* (1900). *An Almanac* and *London Types* had texts by Rudyard Kipling and W. E. Henley respectively, but they were essentially picture books, and the illustrations have since been collected as separate prints. Although these powerful portrayals of late nineteenth-century street folk, sportsmen and animals were cut on wood, they were then lithographed for the books and so printed in greater numbers. Limited editions were produced for the collector market with hand-coloured illustrations. Also published were an ordinary edition, lithographed on cartridge paper with picture boards at 5*s*., an edition on Van Gelder's hand-made paper at 12*s*. 6*d*., and a limited edition printed from wood blocks, coloured by the artist and mounted in a vellum portfolio, selling at £21, a high price indeed! With their grey texture, sharp contrasts and scattered areas of high colour, they look rather like linocuts and have much in common with the posters that preceded them. The silhouetting and high horizons make one think of the Japanese print, but they are more French, a continuation of the tradition of French painter-printers which was enjoying a revival. There is a certain family likeness between the Heinemann productions and, for example, Toulouse-Lautrec's albums, both in point of design and cover typography.

The *Studio* commended certain plates of *London Types*, but found some of the images lacking in clarity, 'Some . . . illustrations contained in this book are less excellent, partly because of a certain confusion in the management of the different planes adopted in the composition, and partly in consequence of a less happy arrangement of the colour tints than is customary in the work of this artist'.[9] *An Alphabet* had mixed reviews at Christmas 1897, the *Artist* considering the illustrations 'original in their imativeness

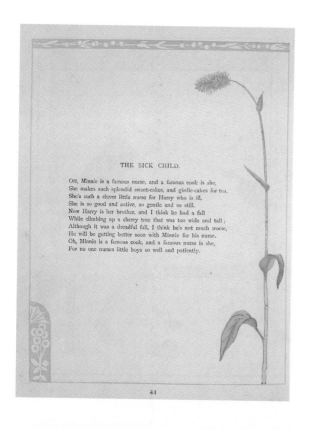

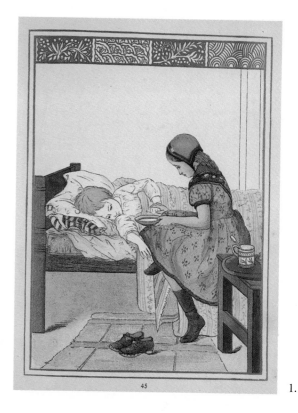

1.

1.

Double page lay-out by J. G. Sowerby (*fl.* 1876–1925) and H. H. Emmerson for *Afternoon Tea* (*c.* 1880). A good example of the 'aesthetic' child's book of the 'Eighties.

2.

2.

'A Gaiety Girl' (*c.* 1895), a poster by Dudley Hardy (1867–1922). Hardy's work reflects the Parisian training of many poster artists of the 'Nineties.

3.

The outer wrapper for the *Pageant*, 1897, designed by Gleeson White
and printed in two colours. A rare survival of a work by the artist
and writer who did so much to create the style of the 'Nineties.
(R. DE BEAUMONT COLLECTION)

4.

4.
'The Queen of The Fishes' by
Lucien Pissarro (1863–1944), a
woodcut from five blocks,
printed in the *Pageant*, 1897.

5.

5.
'Dumas Papa' by E. Gordon
Craig (1872–1966), a coloured
woodcut for the *Dome*, Vol. 2,
January to March, 1899.

BY NICO JUNGMAN

A STREET
BALLET

6.

6.

'A Street Ballet' by Nico Jungmann (1873–1935), printed in
colours in the *Parade*, 1897. An illustration showing the influence of
French poster art.

7.

'The World's Travesties' by Eleanor Fortescue Brickdale
(1871–1945). Signed and dated 1900. Watercolour and
gouache on board. 14 x 16 ¾ ins. (35.6 x 42.5 cm).

8.

'The Princess Lands' by Maurice Greiffenhagen
(1862–1931), 1899. Pen, ink, wash and bodycolour.
12 ¼ x 9 ½ ins.

8.

SWALLOW-MASK SONG OF RHODIAN CHILDREN

9.
Page illustration 'Swallow Mask Song' by Roger Fry (1866–1934),
for *Polyphemus and Other Poems* by R. C. Trevelyan with designs by
R. E. Fry, 1901.

10.

10.
'The Daughter of The Duchess of Canterbury' by E. Gordon Craig
(1872–1966). Signed with monogram and dated 1902. Ink, wash
and slight watercolour. 5 ½ x 6 ins.
(AUTHOR'S COLLECTION)

11.

11.
'Little Bo Peep' by John
Hassall (1868–1948).
Watercolour and ink on
tinted paper. 16 x 14 ins.
(CHRIS BEETLES LTD)

12.

'The Green Purse' by Lewis Baumer (1871–1963). Signed. Black
ink with watercolour and gold. 23 ½ x 19 ½ ins. Dating from about
1895, a very powerful image by a young artist of the 'Nineties.
(CHRIS BEETLES LTD)

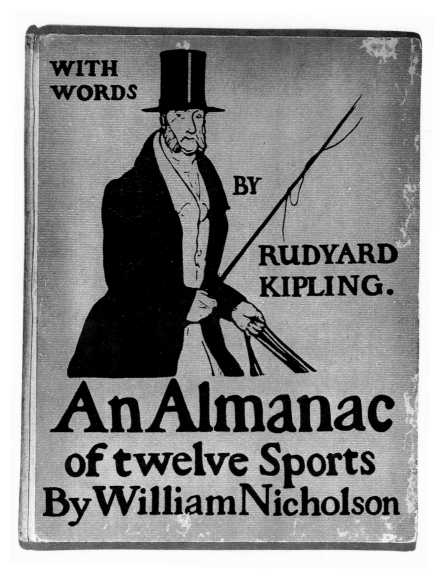

Cover design by William Nicholson (1872–1949) for *An Almanac of Twelve Sports*, 1898.

and of very unequal merit'. The reviewer felt that H for Hen and P for Pig were outstanding, but many others were disappointing, compared to Nicholson's celebrated portrait of Queen Victoria. *The Square Book of Animals*, on the other hand, was a great success and was recommended to the public for 'its peculiar largeness of handling, boldness of touch and straightforward vigour . . .'.[10]

The Twelve Portraits, issued in two series, 1899 and about 1900, consisted of a portfolio of cards with mounted coloured reproductions which derived from the very popular 'Queen Victoria', the Jubilee print of 1897 that Nicholson had done for the *New Review*. The first series included Gladstone, Bismarck and Archbishop Temple in the typically contrasted style of the poster. The much larger 'portfolio', *Characters of Romance* (1900), was seen as a change of style. 'It is notable,' wrote one critic, 'because the drawings are thoroughly individual both in conception and in technique . . . The

'M for Milkmaid' by William Nicholson (1872–1949) for *An Alphabet*, 1898. Lithograph.

broad solid masses, characteristic of Mr Nicholson's early compositions, have given place in the present series to more broken effects, in which a heavy, soft line, akin to that of the reed pen, plays a prominent part in conjunction with colour-washes.'[11] *The Characters*, taken from literature, reflect many aspects of Nicholson's art. Craig called these 'skilful beyond words' in all branches.[12] In his 'Don Quixote' he seems to hark back to his period as poster artist, and in 'Miss Haversham' to the painterly illustrations of Conder, but in 'Commodore Trunnion' he relates to the earlier tradition of Hogarth, and in 'Mr Jorrocks', to that of his great predecessor, the early Victorian illustrator John Leech.

Nicholson's work greatly strengthened this British quality in illustration and although, after 1900, he did not turn his hand to much more than book decorating, he had some notable imitators. Pamela Colman-Smith (*fl.* 1899–1917) was the first to copy the style successfully in her *Widdicombe*

Fair (1899), where the rural characters are portrayed in stumpy black outline. Miss Colman-Smith was later (and very suitably) engaged in producing a series of broadsheets for the Irish private presses of Dun Emer (founded 1903) and the Cuala (founded 1908) for W. B. Yeats and his sister. It is also significant to note that Elkin Matthews, the first partner of John Lane, went on to experiment in broadsheet work as early as 1902. He began publishing rhyme sheets with hand-coloured decorations in the antique style by Jack Yeats, a full ten years before the introduction of the 'Flying Fame' and the advent of Claud Lovat Fraser. Matthews began an Arts and Crafts journal called the *Green Sheaf*, with decorations by Jack Yeats, A.E., and Pamela Colman-Smith. It was an interesting venture, with poetry from John Masefield, and it places Matthews (often thought of as a rather colourless character) in his true perspective. Walford Graham Robertson (1867–1948) also shared the theatrical interests of Craig and

'Baron Munchausen' by William Nicholson (1872–1949) for
Characters of Romance, 1900.

Pryde, and in two early books, *Old English Songs & Dances* (1903) and *A Masque of May Morning* (1904), adapted the Craig style. As late as 1912, Heinemann were still enjoying the bold broadsheet figure when they published W. Dacres Adams' *A Book of Beggars*. A less typical example of the woodblock style is provided by the Paris-trained Alfred Garth Jones, whose boldly engraved work for *The Minor Poems of John Milton* (1898) is half way between the chapbook page and the world of Morris.

The emergence of interest in graphic art and the recognition of the poster largely depended on what was happening on the other side of the Channel. Neither William Nicholson nor James Pryde were much impressed by their brief Parisian training, but their approach to the poster was Gallic. The rise of poster art in the 'Eighties was a French phenomenon, and it was seen as a popular art form where the art gallery was the street and the conoisseurs were ordinary people. The all-important place of letterpress and information was peculiarly British, whereas the Parisian posters integrated word and image in a natural way.

When Henry Davray, a French writer living in London, was asked by Léon Deschamps (editor of the review *La Plume*), to gather together British posters for an exhibition in the mid-1890s, he had a problem.

> I did get some, certainly, and very original ones, too, signed by such artists as Aubrey Beardsley, James Pryde and his brother-in-law, William Nicholson, Maurice Greiffenhagen, and several others, but, in the talks I had with them, they all voiced the same complaint, and that was that the advertisers would insist that the article advertised should be shown in its external packing, as it appeared in the shops . . .[13]

This country was not seriously exposed to the pictorial poster before the Westminster Aquarium exhibition between 1894 and 1896. The great French exponent, Jules Cheret, had learned lithography in this country and there were already British collectors, but with the annual shows the works of Cheret, Anquetin, Bonnard and Steinlen were seen for the first time, and Toulouse-Lautrec actually visited London. The British public were suspicious of innovation and, as F. L. Emanuel was to explain, the new was also the unknown. 'The fact that most of the papers in which these [French] illustrations appear are unknown to, or unpalatable to, the British public, renders it certain that, with but few exceptions, the accomplished work of these modern masters of black and white art will never be as widely appreciated in England as it deserves to be.'[14]

Some of the British woodcuts, with their sharp contrasts, have a lot in common with the work of Félix Vallotton (1865–1925) whose works were being illustrated in the *Studio* by 1896.

Dudley Hardy (1867–1922) was the Paris-trained artist who most benefited from French idioms in his flat-toned, joyous poster style. He at least saw that a poster was not a printed page or a book illustration, but a symbol to be ingested at a glance. His 'Gaiety Girl' owes much to Cheret and is imbued with a Continental effervescence so different from the static mood of the Beggarstaffs. His dancing girls, however, do not seem to have much variety — all pretty things with leg o'mutton sleeves, standing out from a vivid red background. Hardy's earlier work had been for the Savoy Operas: 'The Grand Duke', 'The Grand Duchess', 'His Majesty' and 'The Yeoman of the Guard', the last effective through dramatic outline.

SAMSON

'Samson' by A. Garth Jones (1872–c.1930) for *The Minor Poems of
John Milton*, 1898.

Among Hardy's contemporaries, only a few were totally convincing as
poster makers, or as advertisement designers for the magazines. Aubrey
Beardsley produced a publisher's poster in 1895 in the Japanese 'pillar'
print format, and Raven Hill did an effective silhouetted lady for the
periodical, *Pick Me Up*, at about the same date. Maurice Greiffenhagen did
a similar sun-shaded lady for the *Pall Mall Budget*, but in flat tints and
fugitive outline, closer in manner to the French, but relating to the
Beggarstaffs. The most frequently seen posters were those done for the

'Mr Jacobi receives the Parson and the Painter . . .' by Phil May
(1864–1903) for *The Parson and The Painter*, 1891. Signed. Pen and
ink. 4 ½ x 5 ⅛ ins.
(AUTHOR'S COLLECTION)

theatre, such as John Hassall's 'Vaudeville Theatre A Night Out', in less
stylized figure work, with a fashionable couple welcomed by a waiter.
Beardsley's 'Avenue Theatre' poster of 1894 was still the most sophisticated, forcing the passer-by to look again at the curtained figure to interpret
its meaning. Surprisingly enough, one also finds the very youthful Arthur
Rackham (1867–1939) contributing a very posterish cover to Anthony
Hope's *Dolly Dialogues* (1894).

The poster was now making an impact in the provincial art schools and
was seen as a quick step-ladder to fame and fortune. Lewis Baumer (1870–
1963), who had done little more than illustrate a few childrens' books at
this time, suddenly produced a stunning poster of a lady in a large hat.
The young Alfred Munnings entered for poster competitions in the *Cyclist*
in 1895 and won the gold medal at the Crystal Palace Poster Academy in
1899. This was for an Aldin-like figure of a 'cellist. Typically, Munnings
sold the medal the same evening and went out to dinner on the proceeds!
Munnings won a silver medal at the same show for a tall, narrow poster
of a woman in a Parisian style and in the same year produced 'lovely girls
in large hats' for the Norwich manufacturers of Caley's Chocolates.[15]

The artist whom one would have expected to be most adept at the
poster, because of his brilliant use of space and economy of line, was Phil
May (1864–1903). But apart from a design for his own exhibition of
drawings at the Fine Art Society in 1895, he does not seem to have done

very much publicity work. May's art stands by itself in the 'Nineties and has to be considered as a unique part of the black-and-white revolution.

Phil May was born at Leeds in April 1864 and after attending St George's School there, became an assistant scene painter at the Grand Theatre. This was the perfect beginning for May, who was to remain a lifelong bohemian, mixing in the twilight world of the theatre, the gin palace and the club, peopled by the toffs, topers and flower-girls whom he knew so well. May's important move came in 1883 when he went from Leeds to London to act as assistant artist for *Society* and *St Stephen's Review*, (only recently a fully illustrated journal) contributing theatrical and racing illustrations. In late 1885, May was offered a good opportunity as cartoonist to the *Sydney Bulletin*, an opening that appealed to him. It provided regular employment and a routine, both vital to May's rather feckless character and his indifferent health. May remained in Sydney until the autumn of 1888, although his Australian employer never really understood him and asked for more detailed drawings. May's reply was, 'When I can leave out half the lines I now use I shall want six times the money.'[16] His Australian years, in which he produced some 900 drawings for the *Bulletin*, provided the discipline and professionalism that had previously been lacking. It is also possible that the required speed of work and the less refined printing methods forced May to abbreviate and invent so successfully.

May returned to Europe to study in Rome and Paris, because 'he wanted to improve his drawing'.[17] He shared a studio in Paris's rue Ravignan with Rothenstein, who leaves an account of May that is both sad and revealing:

> Phil somehow managed each week to get his weekly drawings done for *The St Stephen's Review*, and sometimes he sketched at night in cafés and café-concerts, but he did little else. There was no vice in him. He had a touchingly simple and affectionate character, but unfortunately he wasted himself and his means on a crowd of worthless strangers, who setled round his table like flies: while his terrible weakness for drink sapped his will and his physical strength.[18]

May shared models with Rothenstein but spent much more time collecting sketches and ideas for types.

Returning to London, May joined forces with the *St Stephen's Review* again and shortly afterwards began work on his famous series 'The Parson and The Painter'. This was a week-by-week account of the adventures of a country parson, the Rev. Joseph Slapkins, a veritable innocent abroad, and his more sophisticated nephew in London Society. The racy text was by Alfred Allison and, in the course of the saga, the two heroes visited theatres, sporting venues and the seaside, as well as travelling to Boulogne and Paris. May's dashing penwork was the perfect accompaniment to the story. Whistler, a great admirer of May, thought that the diminutive parson was a caricature of Rothenstein!

Although a popular feature in the journal, 'The Parson and The Painter' became a runaway success when it was issued in book form in 1891. At a shilling a time it sold thirty thousand copies at once, although a leading churchman tried to keep it off the railway bookstalls. The slim quarto volume is as far away from the refinements of *fin de siècle* limited editions as it is possible to get, but still very typical of its epoch. Grey paper covers with May's characteristic sketchy heads and script, share the honours with an advertisement for 'Ye Old Cheshire Cheese' and inside, notices about

'Overheard near the Zoo' by Phil May (1864–1903). Signed and
dated 1899. Pen and ink. 11 ¼ x 8 ⅝ ins.
(AUTHOR'S COLLECTION)

The United Nations Club and 'Babadour Cigars' preface the smoky
interiors of May's adventurers. Printed cheaply on ordinary newsprint, the
sharpness of the drawings after more than a hundred years says something
about the resilience of May's technique. His pen work was adapted to
the demands of process printing, which was ideal for reproducing rapid
impressions in half-tone and line work. In 'The Parson and The Painter'
series, the artist is given full rein for sketches, outline and contrasted areas
of black-and-white, augmented by rich parallel hatching in the principal
figures. The formal dress of the day, black coats and top hats, was the
ideal vehicle for bringing out the highlights in hatched line, as is evident
in May's big set-piece illustration, 'The Pelicans At Home'. Equally the
tent-like dresses of ballet girls at the Alhambra, or market girls at stalls,
provide a rhythm of white spaces. But it is only necessary to look at the
original drawings for this series to see that a certain crispness is lost
between the white paper of the design and the toned grey of the newsprint.

May became a famous figure overnight as the result of this humorous series which seemed to symbolise the unbuttoned spirit of the new decade. At the end of 1890 May found himself catapulted into the art department of the newly-founded *Daily Graphic*, which claimed to be the first fully illustrated daily. May was sent to the Chicago World Fair to cover the event and to give readers a pavement view of the Americans. He always worked best under pressure, but this tour was not the success it should have been, the artist's witty but compassionate eye being better attuned to London or Paris. On his return, however, May was able to command almost any commission he liked. He became a regular contributor to the *Sketch*, *Black and White*, the *Daily Chronicle*, the *Pall Mall Budget* and, of course, *Punch*. He also made his appearance in *The Savoy*.

May was a contributor to *Punch* from 1893, and some may think of it as his natural home, but in many respects he was an outsider. *Punch* was conservative to a fault in the 1890s, still printing the quasi-snobbish illustrations of du Maurier and the fine line of the venerable Tenniel. Younger blood in the shape of Bernard Partridge and Raven Hill was coming in, although the more outré work from their pens tended to appear in smaller magazines. May was a bohemian who had entered an exclusive gentleman's club; he behaved himself, but he was different. Because he portrayed the underdog, the street arab, the gin-palace woman with her jug, and the washerwoman, he was often compared to Keene. They certainly shared expertise in draughtsmanship and observation and their subject matter was broadly similar, but there the similarity ended. May's preoccupation with the theatre and the music hall was very different, and most of all he was a born humourist, continually encountering funny situations. Whistler wrote of May, 'There is a lightness and daintiness in what he does combined with knowledge, together with the fact that in his drawings the wit is the artist's, which make a vast difference between him and his contemporaries.'[19]

The seemingly effortless sketches were a combination of concentration and reduction, therefore difficult to imitate. As with so many of the *Punch* artists, working from nature was only part of the process. He collected the 'types' in his sketch-books, gradually whittling them away to bare essentials. Transparent paper was used in the sketch-books to trace backwards from the original study to a simpler and simpler form, removing all the non-essential detail on the way. M. H. Spielmann remarks, 'Indeed, his "economy of means" borders on parsimony.'[20]

Mrs Pennell describes May as the centre of a circle of artists, 'astride his chair, glass in his hand, cigar in his mouth, surrounded by admirers who knew how to converse with his silence'.[21] He was certainly influential, he was important enough to be elected to the *Punch* table at the age of thirty and celebrated enough to have his own *Annuals*. These publications came out regularly between 1892 and 1905 at one shilling each, and were rather flimsy productions in which articles and short stories were strung awkwardly between May's wonderful drawings. Early writers for it included R. H. Sherard, E. F. Benson and Kenneth Grahame, but essentially it was May's showcase, continuing even after his death with posthumous drawings. A small book, *Fun Frolic and Fancy* (1894), was edited by Byron Webber and Phil May; it contained a number of May's chalk character studies, and also many smaller illustrations by his brother Charles

Study of a young girl in black by Phil May (1864–1903), c. 1897.
Pen and ink. 21 x 13 cm.
(CECIL HIGGINS ART GALLERY, BEDFORD)

May. Both these publications have a decidedly popular image and were clearly designed for the railway bookstall.

Any notion that May was only a genius of the reduced line, is entirely dispelled by some of his detailed figure studies. In a remarkable portrait of a young girl, he has modelled the subject, building up tones and textures of a velvet coat with fur trimmings so that both sheen and density are brilliantly captured. The various blacks and greys are carefully balanced, as is the silhouette of hat with ribbons, and the face — a portrait, not a type — is sensitively realised. In this drawing May certainly equals Keene in pure draughtsmanship.

But May's great strengths were in his empathy with the ordinary Londoner and his psychological understanding of the street children. In *Guttersnipes* (1896) and *ABC* (1897), he shows the cheerful and cheeky urchins, and their molls, who laugh and joke about their destitution. In *Phil May's Sketch-Book*, published by Chatto & Windus in 1895, he provides fifty large-scale cartoons in flowing line with spare areas of hatching. This would seem to be a direct copy in size and format of the powerful J. L. Forain albums with their prefaces by Alphonse Daudet, but May's are less biting and less explicit than those of the Frenchman. As F. L. Emanuel was to express it, so neatly, 'The standard of delicacy topples over at such very different angles in England and on the Continent.'[22]

May died of cirrhosis of the liver on 5 August, 1903, at the age of only thirty-nine. Like so many of the stars of the 'Nineties, he seemed unable to survive the period that had given him his fame. He was the perfect foil to his great contemporary Beardsley: where Beardsley was an aesthete, he was a bohemian; where Beardsley concentrated on detail, May concentrated on elimination; where May appealed strongly to a popular audience, Beardsley drew éclat from a sophisticated one. But both men were the victims of their own life style, both concealed their true selves beneath convivial exteriors, both were received into the Roman Catholic Church.

The poster was and remained 'impact illustration'. If it did not catch the interest at once, it had not succeeded — no chance, obviously, to mull over the design as a book lover might. These aspects of the poster, simplification and drama, were reflected in the growing number of coloured picture books at the close of the 'Nineties. Many of the younger artists gained in this over their established colleagues by not having to adapt well-worn styles. The nucleus of the new dynamic group centred upon the London Sketch Club, founded in 1898, a breakaway of the Langham Sketching Society. Phil May was a member, of course, but so too were John Hassall and Tom Browne.

John Hassall (1868–1948) had been trained in Paris and Antwerp, but was first attracted to posters in 1894, going to work for the colour printers, Messrs David Allen & Sons, for a period of seven years. The next forty years, during which he designed hundreds of memorable advertisements, were to see him rise to great heights as a poster artist. Many of his early productions were for theatres and insurance companies, but Hassall succeeded where others failed. In the words of his biographer, 'Added to his fine instinct for decoration, and the mastery which he displays in the handling of broad, flat masses of colour, he possesses in a remarkable degree what one may term the showman's faculty ... Words become unnecessary: the picture tells its own tale.'[23] Hassall also had the great advantage over other artists of being a born humourist, his sense of the comic not being confined to situations, but to the way he expressed them on paper. By the middle 1890s, Hassall was beginning to work on a new book, *Two Well Worn Shoes*, issued in 1899.

Another member of the London Sketch Club, Tom Browne (1872–1910) began as a lace worker in his home town of Nottingham. His talent for drawing led him to be apprenticed to lithographers, and he finally settled in London in 1895. Chiefly influenced by May with his bold outlines, Browne's contrasting black-and-white work is less sophisticated and he uses wider hatching in a less subtle manner. His success began with comics such as *Chips* and he never quite gets away from the comic idiom of fat ladies, cabbies and drunks — he was the precursor of McGill. Browne in fact developed a very good line in show cards and postcards around 1900. His biographer pinpoints the difference between May and Browne:

> Wonderfully sympathetic as the latter [May] was in his portrayal of people, his attitude towards them had a certain intellectual quality of aloofness. He knew them through and through, but as a physician knows his patient. He delighted with unerring touch, to put his finger on their foibles — but always as an onlooker. Tom Browne, too, knows the people inside out, but he views them from their own standpoint.[24]

Browne was a master of the comic strip incident and the action packed series which demanded an impression of constant movement. A recently discovered collection of Browne's preliminary sketches from the archives of his firm, Tom Browne & Co, litho-printers of Nottingham, show the rapidity of his working practice. Browne indicated the movement of an incident with the minimum of lines and with the eye almost of a cinematographer. Presumably May was responsible for this quick-witted reduction of lines but one suspects the admired works of Forain and Steinlen were also important.

One artist who followed a poster style, but who has been overlooked, is the very talented J. W. T. Manuel (d. 1899). An early number of the *Studio*, 1894, devotes two pages to this artist's 'Character Drawings', rapid figure studies of the street, the park and the café, more in outline than in shade, and more in chalk and brush than in pen. They show, to a greater extent than in the work of Browne or Hassall, the direct effect of the French poster on an impressionable young English illustrator; they have rapid observation, movement and humour, worthy of Forain. Manuel worked occasionally for the *Butterfly*, the only magazine where his fresh line would have been at home.

In France, the crowds who flocked to the Paris Exhibition were also buying the popular illustrated humourous weeklies like *Assiette au Beurre* or *Le Rire*, with bold colour covers in a posterish style by Charles Léandre, Abel Faivre and 'Grün', for twenty centimes. Their fluid lithographic style had no counterpart in Britain within the covers of a single magazine. Artists such as Caran d'Ache and Mars were used in London publications, but they were seldom given their head.

Among the French artists who did work in this country, a prominent place should be given to Paul Renouard (1845–1924). He was trained at the Ecole des Beaux-Arts in Paris and worked for magazines such as *Paris Illustré* and *L'Illustration* before moving to England as a principal artist for the *Graphic* in 1884. Renouard worked in England for the next twenty-six years and, like his great contemporary, Alphonse Legros, never managed to learn a word of the language. He was at the height of his powers in the 1890s, making rapid drawings in chalk or pencil, usually of current events or of street characters. He was admired by such varied illustrators as A. S. Hartrick, E. J. Sullivan and James Thorpe. Sullivan wrote of him, 'The excellence of the work of Paul Renouard is dependent largely upon his practice of drawing everything direct from life, and yet, while rarely employing professional models for his purpose, managing to keep the prime

Cover by Grün for *Le Rire*, 24 Octobre 1903.

movement and correct relation throughout a complicated group, no matter what the action.'[25] He often chooses the most unusual viewpoints and uses cut-offs with the effect of a camera. Sullivan considered that his isolation was a huge advantage. 'It is probable', he wrote, 'that much of the strength of Renouard's work in England, Ireland and America arose from the fact that he had to live by his eye so largely, as he spoke little or no English, and that it was thus only by the significance of types and appearances that a subject could make its appeal to him.'[26]

The work of Lucien Pissarro (1863–1944) does not fit into any convenient grouping of the 'Nineties, but his work as a wood-engraver and his French training make it logical to deal with him here among the broadsheet and poster artists. Lucien was the son of the eminent French painter, Camille Pissarro, and grew up in Eragny, where his father was the centre of a group who advocated an unidealised landscape in paint and an anarchist

'The Lord Mayor's Coachman' by Paul Renouard (1845–1924).
Signed with initials. Chalk. 14 x 10 ⅜ ins.
(AUTHOR'S COLLECTION)

philosophy in politics. Lucien was a contributor to the last Impressionist exhibition in 1886. In the 1880s, he had been part of the movement among artists for the revival of the single sheet woodcut in France, a craft reaction not dissimilar to that of Joseph Crawhall here. He had learned English in 1883 and so, in 1890, it was an easy if unusual step for him to settle in London where he became, unintentionally, a mouthpiece for Impressionism.

Lucien Pissarro made contact with the artists of the *Hobby Horse* and the *Dial*: Selwyn Image, Ricketts, Shannon and others. He had already been working with his father on an album, *Les Travaux des Champs* (1889), a sturdy impressionist realist series which reflected his philosophy. Work

A LIST OF BOOKS PRINTED & IN PREPARATION BY E. & L. PISSARRO AT THEIR ERAGNY PRESS & SOLD BY HACON & RICKETTS, 17, CRAVEN ST., STRAND.

PISSARRO

E·ET·L.   LONDON.

ERAGNY PRESS

M.C.M.I.

Prospectus by Lucien Pissarro (1863–1944) for the Eragny Press, 1901.
(R. DE BEAUMONT COLLECTION)

with Ricketts and Shannon led finally, in 1894, to the founding of the Eragny Press. Between then and 1914, Pissarro was to issue thirty-one titles which are unique in the genre of English private press books, having coloured wood-engravings made by the artist. His work for these books remained deliciously Gallic, despite influences from the William Morris printings and a tendency towards the Pre-Raphaelites acquired from Ricketts' *Dial*. The first sixteen Eragny books were produced by Ricketts' Vale Press, but when that ceased in 1904, Eragny continued with a new typeface. Pissarro's first book, *The Queen of the Fishes* (1894), was a Valois fairy tale with hand-written text and this was later followed by texts from

'Les Roses d'Antan' by Lucien Pissarro (1863–1944) for the Eragny
Press, 1896. Pen and ink. 15.7 x 16.7 cm.
(CECIL HIGGINS ART GALLERY, BEDFORD)

Perrault, Flaubert and Villon. 'Les Roses d'Antan' is probably one of
Pissarro's most Pre-Raphaelite blocks, a design that he himself called 'decorative' and which in the borders reflects the influence of Kelmscott. One
wonders whether Eragny also influenced a work of the still young Roger
Fry (1866–1934), his designs for *Polyphemus and Other Poems* (1901).

What Pissarro achieved in these colour wood-engravings was a complete
unity of design, colour and material. In one of his celebrated letters to his
father he writes, 'I want to work directly with the tools without the preliminary drawing, and the wood thus cut will be truly an engraving . . .' He
wanted to work with the material and create something in harmony with
it. As Colin Franklin has recorded, 'Nobody could more thoroughly have
identified himself with the working ideals of a private press.'[27] His work
combined the simple statements of impressionism with the flat tones of
Japanese art, beautifully brought out in clear colours, including gold. In
a memoir by Pissarro printed by Franklin it becomes obvious that the
Eragny Press was neither an economic success nor much supported on
this side of the Channel. Besides this work Pissarro did a certain amount
of illustrating for the anarchist press, notably for Emile Pouget's *Série
Londonienne* (1894–5) and *The Torch* (1895–6). Such diversity was the life
blood of the 'Nineties!

CHAPTER EIGHT

CHILDREN'S BOOKS

*'One who makes pictures for children, like one who writes them stories,
should have the knack of entertaining them . . .'*
GLEESON WHITE

The resurgence of children's illustrated books came twenty years before the *fin de siècle* with the lively art of Richard Doyle in the 1860s and the genius of Walter Crane in the 1870s. Both these artists drew for their young audience in a new way; a feeling of camaraderie and shared experience were manifest in the impish antics of Doyle's creations and in the other-worldly mystery of Crane's.

This emphasis was taken a stage further during the 1890s, and what had been, in those earlier years, delightful or believable, now became intellectually correct and ethically respectable. Romanticism and Pre-Raphaelitism had fostered ancient ballads and popular legends, and both Tennyson and Morris were steeped in this world of antiquity — what they did not find, they invented very convincingly. For the next generation the ancient sagas and stories handed down by verbal tradition had a fresh significance; they were thought to take one back to first principles and, in mysticism and meaning, seemed a good substitute for religion for a growing agnostic readership. It is not insignificant that Sir James George Frazer (1854–1941) first published *The Golden Bough* in 1890, bringing out a second edition in 1900; within the frame of these dates the best illustrated books of legend were produced. Frazer's surprisingly modern approach was to take the study of anthropology as the key factor in understanding man's progress through magic, religion and science. Thus a whole generation of writers and illustrators turned to folklore and myth as a way of understanding their origins.

The illustrated literature of the 'Nineties was thus characterized by a vast diversity of source; not only the traditional stories of the British Isles, but also the folklore of all the continents, were ransacked for new material. Rudyard Kipling's charming Indian stories are only one example of this; the re-told French, German, Norse and Russian legends are another. Beautifully illustrated, and treated with a high seriousness, some of these books must have appealed as much to adults as to their charges. Frazer's ideas were so very much in the wind.

It is strange, therefore, that though the 'Nineties was a remarkable period in the nursery library and especially in the design and physical appearance of children's books, there is no single illustrator comparable with an Arthur Hughes in the 1860s or an Arthur Rackham in the 1900s. Almost all illustrated children's fiction reached a remarkably high standard, and publishers seemed to compete for ever more dazzling effects and beguiling fancies with the artists they employed. But the richness and variety originated in an earlier period.

It was in the 1890s that the importance of early children's publications was first recognised. There was the appearance of E. M. Field's *The Child and His Book* (1891) and of the influential and attractive *Pages and Pictures From Forgotten Children's Books* (1898–9) from the Leadenhall Press. A realisation that the juvenile library of the past had something to teach the present, resulted in a spate of books that imitated the old works of Newbery of St Paul's Church Yard, the celebrated children's publisher. These new books were similar in everything but content; pastiches multiplied and aesthetic antiquarianism became the vogue. The value of early children's books increased gradually and in the 1890s leading publishers like Elkin Matthews became collectors of the juvenile works of the eighteenth century.

The improvement in child literature really dates from the middle of the nineteenth century and most of the contemporary writers of the 'Nineties put the resurgence down to two factors: the Great Exhibition of 1851 and 'Felix Summerley'. The Exhibition focussed attention on new techniques in paper, printing and binding, that would make books for the young more attractive and more economical to produce. 'Felix Summerley', the pen name of Henry Cole, afterwards director of the South Kensington Museum, was synonymous with good design and a more advanced view of what a children's book should be. It was largely due to him that the new books were *for* children rather than about them, and that the heavy moralising was replaced by a lighter touch because the child was supposed to enjoy his reading. In the 1840s some very charming illustrated books had been produced; they were precursors of those of the 1860s, a time when publishers began to market books on the strength of pictures alone.

The productions of such firms as Routledge meant a revolution in the style and quality of children's books, but even so, publishers were reaching only a fairly well-off, middle-class readership. After the passing of the Education Act in 1870 and the subsequent Act for compulsory education in 1876, a whole new audience opened up for aspiring artists and writers, and publishers began issuing cheap imitations of what had gone before, in garish lithography and on execrable papers.

The Routledge 'Toy Books' (touched on in Chapter Three) are the quintessential Victorian pictured page; they deserve a mention here because they enjoyed a long span from 1865, and were still being reprinted in 1900. Walter Crane designed two or three toy books a year between 1865 and 1876 for the Sixpenny Series; the format was always eight colour-printed pages and a colour-printed cover, and the cost was 6*d.* for paper covers or 1*s.* for linen. All the toy books were printed from wood-engraved blocks, supervised by Edmund Evans.

By 1870 Crane had succeeded in creating a totally individual style for children, based on the Japanese prints that he so much admired. He also literally carved a place for the illustrator, giving his own name to the series,

'Walter Crane's Toy Books', and having it printed on the cover, which was unusual in children's publishing at this time. This series was followed in 1874–6 by the Shilling 'Toy Books' in a quarto format but with separate text pages instead of texts in the picture space, a Crane mannerism. The picture pages of *The Frog Prince* and *Beauty and The Beast* are filled to capacity with decorative effect and incident, an aesthetic overflow which is partly a debt from the Pre-Raphaelites, and one that was to be taken up with a vengeance in the 'Nineties.

Even in 1897, Gleeson White could write of a dearth of coloured picture books and hold Crane's models up as a shining example. 'For as a maker of children's books, no one ever attempted the task he fulfilled so gaily, and no one since has beaten him on his own ground. Even Mr Howard Pyle, his most worthy rival, has given us no wealth of colour prints. So that the famous toy books still retain their well-merited position as the most delightful books for the nursery and the studio, equally beloved by babies and artists.'[1] Ever watchful of fashion, John Lane realised that by re-issuing them (which he did, 1895–7) he would fill a gap in the market. Crane bought the original wood-engraved blocks from Routledge in 1894 and Lane published the series the following year, with new title-pages and endpapers designed by Crane.

'Curly Locks' by Kate Greenaway (1846–1901) for *The April Baby's Book of Tunes*, 1900. Watercolour. This was Kate Greenaway's last book which she had worked on in the 'Nineties.

(SOTHEBY'S)

Edmund Evans was also the begetter of Randolph Caldecott and Kate Greenaway, in that he recognised their genius and was prepared to give their work the quality of printing and supervision that it deserved. Caldecott was dead by 1885 so his work falls outside our period, but both Crane and Greenaway continued to produce illustrated books for children in the 'Nineties, although they cannot be called typical of those years. The Greenaway *Annuals* still appeared during the age of *The Yellow Book*, the only connection being their common origins in aestheticism. Walter Crane produced two of his most attractive volumes, *Flora's Feast: a Masque of Flowers* in 1889 and *Queen Summer* in 1891, but they are hardly children's fare. Also, within our period, he illustrated two undoubted juveniles, *Steps to Reading* and *The Walter Crane Infant Reader* (1898), both by Nellie Dale. Crane's contribution to the new generation of author-illustrators was in his design of the page, the positive way the text was incorporated within the picture, the manner in which the volumes — such as *The Baby's Opera* (1877) — were finely balanced, and the novelty of including music.

It would be a mistake, though, to think that the prelude to the 'Nineties was dominated by these artists. Warne's in particular were producing excellent picture books: Gleeson White specially commended *Afternoon Tea* (1880), which 'set a new fashion for "aesthetic" little quartos costing five or six shillings each'.[2] The illustrations are by J. G. Sowerby (*fl.* 1876–1925), the stained glass artist, and H. H. Emmerson. The muted colours and very careful page lay-out are typical of aestheticism and foreshadow the kind of preciosity that was to develop in *fin de siècle* juvenile publishing. This book was followed by *At Home* (1881), *At Home Again* (1886) and *Young Maids and Old China* (n.d.). The firms of Griffiths and Farran, Gardner, Darton & Co, Hildesheimer and Dean were all issuing very attractive coloured story-books. Marcus Ward produced such titles as *The Robbers Cave* and *Nursery Numbers*, illustrated by A. M. Lockyer, who also illustrated *Bubbles*, giving it a strongly Japonesque cover although the story is about cats and mice.

Other illustrators who contributed good work to this plethora of books are Mrs Houghton, T. Pym and R. Andre, the last supplying well illustrated books for the religious press, especially works by Horatia Ewing. Linley Sambourne (1844–1910) is principally remembered as a *Punch* artist, but he illustrated the *New Sandford and Merton* (1872) and *The Royal Umbrella* (1888), displaying his talent for humour. But his most influential work must be the celebrated edition of *The Water Babies* by Charles Kingsley (1886). This set a style for sweeping penmanship in black-and-white, and imaginative decoration of the page, which was not common before.

Kate Greenaway's works were perennially popular, but by 1890 were probably considered a little anaemic by the younger illustrators; even her supporter, Ruskin, felt that they were painted in 'camomile tea'. Writing in 1897, Gleeson White noted,

> The art of Miss Greenaway is part of the legend of the aesthetic craze, and while its storks and sunflowers have faded, and some of its eccentricities are forgotten, the quaint little pictures on Christmas cards, in toy books, and elsewhere, are safely installed as items of the art product of the century. Indeed, many a popular Royal Academy picture is likely to be forgotten before the illustrations from her hand.[3]

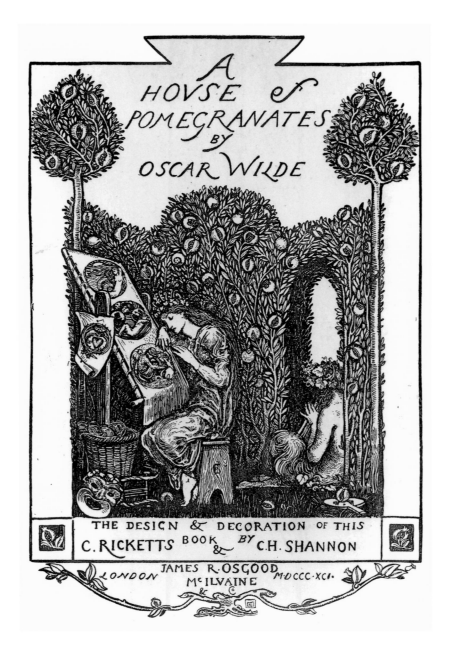

Title-page by Charles Ricketts (1866–1931) and Charles Shannon
(1863–1937) for *A House of Pomegranates* by Oscar Wilde, 1891.

The 'Nineties style was really introduced into children's literature in 1888. That was the year that Oscar Wilde produced his masterpiece *The Happy Prince and Other Tales*. This contained five fairy stories, the most celebrated being 'The Selfish Giant' and 'The Remarkable Rocket'. The illustrators were Walter Crane and G. P. Jacomb Hood whose work may perhaps have helped the stories achieve the instant success they gained. Oscar Wildes's second attempt was *A House of Pomegranates* (1891), which was a less satisfactory selection of stories, although the book itself should have been a beautiful production. The price of a children's book at twenty-one shillings was far too high, the greyness of the illustrations was not striking, and the artists, Ricketts and Shannon, were not really story-book

THE FISHER-
-MAN AND
HIS SOVL

TO H.S.H.
ALICE, PRINCESS
OF MONACO.

Every evening
the young Fisherman
went out upon the
sea, and threw his
nets into the water.
When the wind
blew from the land he caught nothing, or but
little at best, for it was a bitter and black-
winged wind, and rough
waves rose up to meet it.
But when the wind blew to
the shore, the fish came in

63

The Young King.

in the heart of the
pearl." And he told
them his three dreams.
And when the cour-
tiers heard them they
looked at each other
and whispered, saying :
"Surely he is mad ; for
what is a dream but a
dream, and a vision
but a vision ? They
are not real things that
one should heed them.
And what have we to
do with the lives of
those who toil for us ?
Shall a man not eat
bread till he has seen
the sower, nor drink
wine till he has talked
with the vinedresser ?"
And the Cham-
berlain spake to
the young King,
and said, " My
lord, I pray thee
set aside these
black thoughts
of thine, and put

19

Title-page by Ricketts and Shannon for a story in *A House of Pomegranates* by Oscar Wilde, 1891.

Page decoration by Ricketts and Shannon for *A House of Pomegranates* by Oscar Wilde, 1891.

illustrators. This all goes to prove that what children want is not necessarily high art! The volume was eventually remaindered, although it is still much sought after today.

More typical of the new epoch were the story-books of Andrew Lang (1844–1912), the essayist and classicist. He seems an unlikely figure for this role and critics considered him to be a jack of all trades and therefore rather second rate, but his books were immensely popular. He belongs to the same class of Victorian intellectual as Frazer; fleeing, like Frazer, from religion to myth he acquired on the way a fair knowledge of anthropology and psychical research. He began with *The Blue Fairy Book* in 1889 and these 'coloured' offerings were to appear every Christmas, making altogether a score of volumes. In each one, Lang re-told popular magical stories from around the world. Mrs Lang and their daughter gathered in the material, Lang sifted and arranged it and H. J. Ford illustrated it. Henry Justice Ford (1860–1941) was a prolific illustrator and, as a classical scholar himself, a good enough match for Lang. His training under Alphonse Legros and later under Herkomer gave him a precision in drawing that was well suited to the line block of the 'Nineties. As a friend of Burne-Jones, Ford gained insights into the more painterly aspects of myth

BENSURDATU ATTACKS THE SEVEN-HEADED SERPENT.

'Bensurdatu attacks the Seven-Headed Serpent' by H. J. Ford
(1860–1941) for *The Grey Fairy Book* by Andrew Lang, 1900.

and legend, enabling him to encompass a great deal of detail and incident
in the rather small pages of Lang's books. In his first fairy books there are
distinctive influences of Crane both in figures and in expressions, but
towards the end of the century, and particularly in the eastern legends,
there is a real influence from Boyd Houghton and that artist's *Arabian
Nights*. His illustration 'The Gift of Fortune', in *The Grey Fairy Book* (1900),
is pure Burne-Jones in its dreamy quality and low sight line; elsewhere
the goblins of Doyle seem to obtrude. The illustrations complement the
text, but rarely seem to flow towards it in the Charles Robinson style.
Ford's most characteristic period mannerisms are the *art-nouveau* frames of
the pictures, the labels in hand script, and the occasional vignette, but he
steers away from initials and tailpieces. Ford also shows himself, in *The
Animal Story Book* (1896), to be an accomplished natural history draughtsman, the illustrations including bears, wolves, snakes and buzzards. His
superb asymmetrical covers, gold-blocked on cloth, are among the best
things of their kind; a stark oriental mountain lion, or a witch on an owl's
back, immediately arrests the attention.

Thomas Balston, who thought these books 'solid', had a word to say
about the covers. 'It was perhaps the brightness of the bindings rather
than the monotonous illustrations which made the annual appearance of
one or two volumes a matter of such interest in nurseries and schoolrooms.
Children were all agog to see a *Pink Fairy Book*, 1897, for instance, after

'Udea found lifeless by her Seven Brothers' by H. J. Ford (1860–
1941) for *The Grey Fairy Book* by Andrew Lang, 1900.

blue and red and green and yellow had been exhausted; they had never
seen a pink book before.'[4]

Gleeson White, referring to Ford's one-man show at the Fine Art
Society in May 1895, mentioned the artist's popularity even with the critics,
but had two reservations. He considered that the illustrations lost much in
their reduction for the fairy books, the originals being four times the size,
and that they were too busy. 'His work is full of imagination, full of detail;
perhaps at times a little overcrowded, to the extent of confusion.'[5]

In the same league is John Dixon Batten (1860–1932), a prolific illustrator from the same intellectual background and, like Ford, a pupil of

ORPHEVS·AND·MEDEA·CHARM
THE·SNAKE·THAT·GVARDS·THE
GOLDEN·FLEECE·

'Orpheus and Medea' by J.D. Batten (1860–1932) for *The Book of
Wonder Voyages*, 1896.

Legros. Batten's best work is probably represented in another series of
fairy books in which he collaborated with the compiler Joseph Jacobs.
English Fairy Tales (1890), *Celtic Fairy Tales* (1892), *Indian Fairy Tales*
(1893), *More English Fairy Tales* (1894) and *The Book of Wonder Voyages*
(1896). Batten presents greater contrast in his black-and-white work than
Ford; some of the pages have a rich texture of blacks, others are almost
pure line. In this I think he has the edge on Ford, as also in his more
purely imaginative vein, and in the strain of humour that comes through
his drawings. White, writing of Batten, refers to 'the fertility of his invention and his consistent improvement in technique'.[6] Some of these books
were produced in limited editions with hand-coloured illustrations on Japanese vellum. Batten was something of an innovator, developing his own

East o' the Sun & West o' the Moon

'John and the Swan Maiden' by J. D. Batten (1860–1932) for an
unidentified edition of William Morris's *Earthly Paradise, c.* 1895.
Pen and ink. 12 x 8 ½ ins (50.5 x 21.5 cm).
(AUTHOR'S COLLECTION)

way of colour printing from wood-blocks according to the Japanese method.[7] He was very much part of the Burne-Jones circle and had as his patrons the Earl of Carlisle, a Pre-Raphaelite and socialist, and his wife.

Another sage writing for infant minds was Judge Parry, who produced three bestsellers during our period, *Katawampus* (1895), *Butterscotia* (1896) and *The First Book of Krab* (1897). All three were illustrated by the otherwise unknown sculptor and illustrator, Archie Macgregor, and published by David Nutt. One can see a sculptural sense in Macgregor's work, a beautiful modelling of figures and a weaving of fact and fantasy to be found in *art nouveau* bronzes. The ordinary edition of *Katawampus* is handsome, but another edition, limited to sixty copies signed by the author, is especially handsome. This was produced in a cream vellum cover with gilding, and with the frontispiece and last page printed in green.

Very few of the folk-tales garnered from distant lands were illustrated in a way that paid any respect to the culture or traditions of those countries. Artists seemed to think that a few props and a token gesture to the landscape were sufficient. One of the few exceptions to this chauvinistic policy was John Lockwood Kipling (1837–1911), the father of Rudyard Kipling. He was for many years the principal of the Mayo School of Art at Lahore (1865–75), and afterwards Curator of the Central Museum at Lahore until 1893. Deeply versed in the culture and art of India, and a brother-in-law of Sir Edward Burne-Jones, he was well placed to bridge the artistic divide. He was an able and imaginative black-and-white artist and his illustrations to Flora A. Steel's *Tales of the Punjab* (1894), use Indian forms and imagery in a truly imaginative way. At the same time he was illustrating his son's *The Jungle Book* (1894) and *The Second Jungle Book* (1895). Rudyard Kipling was to illustrate his own *Just So Stories for Little Children* in 1902 with equal imagination if less sureness of touch, the feeling for Mogul art and culture being far less evident than in his father's work.

An illustrator who in many ways epitomises the flow and flourish of the 1890s in his curvilinear designs and inventiveness is Charles Robinson (1870–1937). The middle son in the Robinson triumvirate, with Thomas and William Heath, he was born into the world of engraving and illustration that had occupied his family for two generations. An occasional student at various art schools, but more at home in the bohemian world of Fleet Street, Robinson assimilated something from the Arts and Crafts tradition of Crane, a liking for the microscopic detail from the Pre-Raphaelites, and even some of the fantasy of Doyle and Tenniel. Primarily a decorative artist whose work was an integral part of the whole book, Robinson did not slavishly imitate any of the geniuses of the day. He was commended once for being neither a Beardsley, nor a Ricketts nor an Anning Bell. His pictures were never sinister like Beardsley's, serious like Ricketts' or sophisticated in the manner of Bell.[8]

The choice of Robinson in 1895 to illustrate Robert Louis Stevenson's *A Child's Garden of Verses* made his name, for the world he portrayed was both aesthetic and innocent. Gleeson White at once hailed a new discovery: 'one of the youngest recruits to the army of illustrators, and yet his few years' record is both lengthy and kept at a singularly high level'. He goes on to analyse the 'sign-manual' of the Robinson style. 'In the first of his designs which attracted attention, we find the half-grotesque, half-real child that he has made his own — fat, merry little people, that are bubbling

Illustration by J. Lockwood Kipling (1837–1911) for *Tales of The
Punjab* by Flora A. Steel (Macmillan), 1894.
(SOTHEBY'S)

over with joy of mere existence.'[9] Walter Crane also gave him high praise:
'He shows quaint and sometimes weird fancy, a love of fantastic architecture, and is not afraid of outline and large white spaces'.[10] *A Child's Garden
of Verses* does owe a little to Beardsley in stippling effects and symbolism,
but *King Longbeard* of 1898, with its heavily patterned pages and rich
borderings, is a tribute to Crane, and indirectly to Morris. Robinson was
well served by the Bodley Head for whom he designed ten titles between
1895 and 1900, and he was a guest at John Lane's celebrated smoking

'King Herla' by Charles Robinson (1871–1937) for *True Annals of Fairy Land* (Dent), 1900. Pen and ink.
(SOTHEBY'S)

parties.[11] Dent's, Bell's and Darton's all played a part in promoting his work, with titles ranging from *Fairy Tales From Hans Christian Andersen* (1899) to *Sintram and His Companions* (1900). A complete parody of the Beardsley style was produced by him in 1896 entitled *Christmas Dreams* by Awfly Weirdly which demonstrated his remarkable versatility.

Robinson excelled at cover designs and this talent is best borne out by the decoration of the gift-books or Christmas books for children brought out by the Bodley Head and Dent's in the mid-'Nineties. The great difference between these annuals and those of ten or twenty years earlier, was that they were designed throughout, great care being taken that binding, endpapers, fly-leaves and half-titles should blend well together. Part of this success was the fact that, since the 1880s, cover designs had become more and more the province of the publishers rather than the binders, and ultimately, therefore, of the artists themselves.

The late Victorian years were, of course, the period of illustrated children's magazines: *Little Folks*, the *Boy's Own Paper* and others. Although attractive, they do not have the authentic stamp of the *fin de siècle* upon them, as do individual children's books.

One of the most interesting experiments in the realm of children's illustrations in the 'Nineties was the *Parade*, a handsome annual that is sometimes classed as a magazine, although it only appeared once. It is the product of much careful thought, as is obvious from the printed cloth covers and the endpapers, the page design and the decorations. It was edited by the doyen of the 'Nineties book, Gleeson White, who probably had extensive co-operation from Paul Woodroffe. It is his repeating patterns, of drummer boys on the endpapers and child knights, riding through a sea of scrolls, on the cover, that give the volume its distinctive aesthetic appeal. Aubrey Beardsley designed the title-page of arabesques (nothing sinister here for the boys and girls) and the two-colour frontispiece is by Mrs Percy Dearmer. Thereafter, most of the star performers of the period appear: Charles Robinson decorating a Le Gallienne poem, Léon Solon with a monumental tailpiece, and Alan Wright with a series of studiedly aesthetic interiors. Paul Woodroffe decorates an attractive musical score and Laurence Housman one of his own enchanted stories, 'The Fire-Eaters'. Some extremely strong fairy illustration comes from Nico Jungmann, then only twenty-four years old, in the form of five plates for 'The

'Ride a Cock Horse' by Paul Woodroffe (1875–1945) for *A Second Book of Nursery Rhymes*; music by Joseph Moorat (Allen), 1896.

Fairy illustration by Alfred Garth Jones (1872–*c*.1930 for an
unidentified book.

Changing Years', and L. de Montmorency provides a last burst of Pre-
Raphaelitism with 'Princess Zezolla'. Interestingly enough, it is Nico Jungmann's one-colour plate, 'A Street Ballet', that really captures the spirit of
the book; it has all the lightness and freedom of French poster art.

Elsewhere there are excellent things: Alfred (Garth) Jones' 'Voyage to
Fairy Land' is in the broader woodcut style, denoting his love of Dürer
and A. Van Anrooy, an occasional illustrator, gives some delicate penwork,
more in the style of the *Boys's Own Paper*. But the real surprise is Max
Beerbohm as an illustrator of childhood. His own tale, 'The Story of

The Small Boy And The Barley-Sugar', is enlivened by brilliantly simple drawings with the caricaturist's effortless control of line and expression.

The *Parade* is an interesting phenomenon. Was Gleeson White trying to prove something, or attempting to inculcate his good taste in younger readers at an early age? So many gift-books fail because of patchiness, but this one works because the text has an unusual preponderance of writer-illustrators: Housman, Mrs Dearmer, Max Beerbohm, Starr Wood and Alfred Jones. All this is thoughtfully arranged. Links are provided by the initials and decorations of W. J. Overnell and L. de Montmorency. This successful arrangement was never repeated. Strangely enough the book is not common; I have only seen two copies in twenty years. The *Studio*, usually hard to please, called the volume 'sumptuous' and particularly liked Woodroffe's 'admirable designs for the cover and end-papers of this comely book'.[12] It is a curious fact that James Thorpe makes no mention at all of the *Parade* in his book on the 'Nineties.

Robert Anning Bell (1863–1933) was not primarily a child's illustrator, but he launched his career with a number of children's books: *Jack The Giant Killer, Cinderella,* and *Beauty and The Beast* (all 1894). In 1901 he was to illustrate an edition of *Grimm's Household Tales.* An Arts and Crafts artist, brought up in the tradition of Crane, Anning Bell makes few concessions to childhood in *Household Tales.* The classical, almost Renaissance, scenes

'Briar Rose' by Robert Anning Bell (1863–1933) for *Grimm's Household Tales* (Dent), 1901.

are set in two dimensions like a frieze, perhaps an inheritance from his work as a stained glass designer and muralist. Crane considered him at the head of the new school, 'He has evidently studied the early printers and book decorators in outline of Venice and Florence to some purpose; by no means merely imitatively, but with his own type of figure and face, and fresh natural impressions . . .'.[12] Gleeson White deplored the publishers' scant use in this field of Bell's work which, apart from the *Grimm*, was limited to minor titles. 'It is singular,' he wrote, 'that the fancy of Mr Anning Bell which seems exactly calculated to attract a child and its parent at the same time has not been more frequently requisitioned for this purpose.'[13]

Anning Bell was quite widely used by the firm of J. M. Dent, and this seems a reasonable place to consider the leading publishers of children's books. It seems that Dent, on the strength of Beardsley's involvement alone, was ranked as an avant-garde book publisher. But J. M. Dent's memoirs, published in 1938, make very little of their 'Nineties illustrators and their extensive lists of children's books. Dent's acquisition of Beardsley for the *Morte d'Arthur* had been a happy accident rather than a consummate choice, although to give him his due he did regard the work as 'a new breath of life in English black-and-white drawing'.[14] The first drawing prepared for Dent's approval had been 'The Achieving of the Sangreal', which the publisher called a masterpiece and of which he was still 'the proud possessor' in 1921.[15] To their credit, Dent's decided to hold an exhibition of all the black-and-white work done for the firm and staged this in the rooms of the Institute of Watercolour Painters, Piccadilly in September and October, 1894. Dent states that he included work by J. D. Batten, R. Anning Bell, Arthur Rackham and Walter Crane, but some of it did not live up to expectations. Enough public interest was generated, however, to put forward suggestions for new books, and their illustrated work was greatly extended.

When the Dent archives were sold at several Sotheby's sales between 1987 and 1990[16], it was possible to discover which artists the firm was using at the turn of the century. Apart from the artists already mentioned, there was Charles Robinson, who contributed a remarkable group of drawings for *The Adventures of Odysseus*, *Sintram and His Companions* (both 1900) and *The Reign of King Oberon* (1902), and Thomas Heath Robinson (*c.*1869–1950), who produced attractive work, including drawings for Charles Kingsley's *The Heroes* (1899) and *Fairy Tales From The Arabian Nights* of the same year. The young Arthur Rackham was employed very early on, in 1896, to illustrate S. J. Adair Fitzgerald's *The Zankiwank and the Blether-witch*. This work, in a less full-blooded colour than later Rackham, has all his humour, movement and caprice in embryo form.

Among the other charming illustrations used, one should name Patten Wilson's series of crowded ink drawings for *A Child's History of England* by Charles Dickens (1902) and *Stories of Early British Heroes* (also 1902).

One of the most delightful, though now forgotten, illustrators in this field was Winifred Green (afterwards Graham). Dent's used her to illustrate Charles and Mary Lamb's *Mrs Leicester's School* (1899), a companion volume to *Poetry For Children* which had appeared the previous year. Winifred Green borrows much from Kate Greenaway but her figures and decoration are a little more forceful.

'Au Clair de la Lune' by Thomas Heath Robinson (*c.* 1869–1950)
for *A Book of French Songs For The Young* by Bernard Minnsen (Dent),
1899. Pen and ink.
(SOTHEBY'S)

Perhaps the most engaging of all Dent's small format children's books are those in the Banbury Cross series, edited by Grace Rhys. Dent's were as particular about these twelve juveniles as they were about their classics: each diminutive volume in green or red cloth had a silk tie, and the cover design was blocked in gold. The cover would be designed by the artist, who would also illustrate the entire book. As to the choice of artist, this would usually fall on a member of the younger generation who was being noticed in the *Studio*.

The series includes *Banbury Cross and Other Nursery Rhymes*, illustrated by Alice B. Woodward (1862–1911) in her rather linear style, with its clear areas of white against black and its friendly fantasy. Crane commends

Illustration by Winifred Green (*fl.* 1899–1902) for *Mrs Leicester's
School* by Charles and Mary Lamb (Dent), 1899. Pen and ink.
(SOTHEBY'S)

her for her medievalism, Gleeson White for her 'amazing humour'.[17] A
score of books were illustrated by her in pen and watercolour, and I have
also seen a series of serious drawings of prehistoric animals, perhaps for a
school book, showing her as no mean artist. Also in the series is a delightful
Ali Baba And The Forty Thieves with finely executed work by H. Granville
Fell (1872–1951), a lively and amusing *Aesop's Fables* from Charles Robinson and a gentle *The House That Jack Built* by Violet M. Holden (1872–
1939). This artist, sister of the celebrated and over-rated diary writer,
Edith B. Holden, flaunts her Birmingham training in the woodcut style of
her little landscapes and the Dutch doll appearance of her figures. (See
page *iv*)

Another important publisher of childrens' books was Lawrence &
Bullen. They made the rather surprising choice of William Strang for two
superb titles in 1895–6, and Strang collaborated with J. B. Clark (b. 1857),
yet another Legros student. The books were *The Surprising Adventures of
Baron Munchausen* (1895) and *Sinbad The Sailor and Alibaba and The Forty
Thieves* (1896). Strang's attitude to illustration was ambivalent; he was
never interested in merely following a text and sought for much greater
freedom of expression. The reproductions here were in zincograph with
their careful play of black-and-white areas deriving from the Japanese
print. Although they may not have suited the artist greatly, they are mas-

The four-and-twenty sailors
   That stood between the decks
Were four-and-twenty white mice,
   With chains about their necks.

The captain was a duck,
   With a jacket on his back ;
When the ship began to move,
   The captain said, " Quack ! quack ! "

Page opening by Alice B. Woodward (1862–1911) for *Nursery Rhymes* in the Banbury Cross series (Dent), 1895.

terly examples of their period, capturing that blend of new technique with old tradition that made the 'Nineties so exciting. Both books represent a remarkable synthesis of style between Clark and Strang, although they are so different from the latter's serious work. Strang also produced a woodcut *Book of Giants* for the Unicorn Press in 1898 with twenty-five copies hand-coloured by the artist.

If Lawrence & Bullen were in the vanguard of the new children's book with their choice of illustrator and designer, the firm of David Nutt epitom-ised the vogue of a new style in old clothes: the appeal of the woodcut book of the eighteenth century brought up to date. Within ten years of the Leadenhall Press issuing Crawhall's *Old Aunt Elspa's ABC*, described as 'outrageously quaint', Nutt was doing similar things in a less idiosyncratic guise. *Good Night* by Dollie Radford (1895), was illustrated with designs by Louis Davis in a naïve style and coloured by hand. Their whimsical manner clearly anticipates the work of Lovat Fraser by about twenty years. Gleeson White calls them 'dainty in their quality, and tender in their poetic

Illustration by H. Granville Fell (1872–1951) for *Ali Baba And The
Forty Thieves* for the Banbury Cross series (Dent), 1895.

Frontispiece and title-page by Violet M. (1872–1939) and Evelyn
Holden (1877–1968) for *The House That Jack Built* in the Banbury
Cross series (Dent), 1895.

interpretation of child-life'.[18] David Nutt is also the imprint for another interesting book, *Nursery Songs and Rhymes of England*, illustrated by Winifred Smith, who died very young. Her earlier work was *Children's Singing Games* (two volumes), all in the conventional Birmingham School of Art idiom in which she was trained. Some copies of this book are hand-coloured by the colourist, Gloria Cardew. Similarly, another Dollie Radford title, *Songs For Somebody* (1893), has colour illustrations by Gertrude Bradley, supervised by that magician among colour printers, Edmund Evans, at his premises in Racquet Court, Fleet Street.

Evans was also involved in some of the colour print books of F. D. Bedford (1864–1954), who had already drawn a splendid series for Methuen, *The Battle of the Frogs and Mice* (1894). He repeated his success with the gem-like colours of *A Book of Nursery Rhymes* for the same publisher.

Bedford was one of the first really to benefit from the advent of the new colour work, an innovation that was part of the *fin de siècle*, but was to flower in the later Edwardian years. The half-tone, perfected around 1893, had greatly changed the appearance of magazines — though never of the quality black-and-white book — and now, before the turn of the century, the half-tone three and four-colour process was achieving satisfactory results. Because, in its original form, it presented a mass of dots, which translated an image rather than accurately reproducing it, the books from the new process looked very different. J. M. Dent recalled this:

> In the year 1900 the three colour process gave us a more effective means of reproducing colour work in our books. It had often been tried in previous years, but by this year more progress had been made and a deal of crudeness eliminated by careful etching, which requires almost as great a skill as hand etching and even more attention to minutiae in 'biting'. I have mentioned that my son John had begun business as a photo-etcher some years before, and he at once began to produce the best work possible in this direction.[19]

There were a number of interesting large watercolours produced at this time, only revealed at the dispersal of the Dent archives in 1987–8.[20] They included four superb illustrations by E. J. and C. M. Detmold for *Pictures From Birdland* (1899), when those prodigies were only fifteen years old! There was a Charles Robinson watercolour for *The Adventures of Odysseus*, already mentioned, and some elaborately coloured fairy subjects, dated 1901, by Arthur Rackham, but not for any identifiable book. This suggests considerable experiment and uncertainty at this time as to whether the colour market was actually going to leap forward. Another series of drawings by Rackham for the *Zankiwank* book of 1896 had been produced in ink and then coloured by Rackham, possibly for a project that was abandoned. The dispersal sale also included a full-page watercolour by Mabel Chadburn, in a late Greenaway style, for her *The Fairy Bird and Piggy Wig* which was issued in 1905. By this date the colour market for children's fiction was well under way.

Dent's colour books were not alone. 'What were called Colour Books poured out from Macmillan as they did from every other publisher at that time.'[21] Hugh Thomson was Macmillan's star performer and in 1898, perhaps with the intention of using his name as successfully as Crane's, the firm launched 'Hugh Thomson's Fairy Books'. These began with *Jack*

The Giant Killer, a delightful production with sixteen magnificent full-page colour illustrations by Thomson. They prove how excellent his talent and colouring were, although nowhere near as imaginative as Rackham's. Sadly, this book was the only one in the series to be issued, although the artist had projected a *Cinderella* to accompany it and had made a tour of pantomimes for inspiration.[22] It was frequently said that Thomson's giant was too frightening for the nursery, a complaint that seems a far cry from mid-Victorian attitudes; perhaps Macmillan's felt that this was not their market. (See page *ii*)

John Lane, who had re-issued the 'Toy Books', produced some attractive new books at the Bodley Head at this time. Examples include *Wymps and Other Fairy Tales*, illustrated by Mrs Mabel Dearmer with coloured boards, and the later *A Hundred Fables of Aesop* (1903) with many full-page pictures by P. J. Billinghurst. Some publishers, like Warne's in *The Bunkum Book* (1900), contented themselves simply with a coloured frontispiece by Maud Trelawney; there were others like Longman's, who gave thirty coloured plates to the highly popular *Golliwog* series, invented and drawn by Florence K. Upton in 1901.

Illustration by Hugh Thomson (1860–1920) for *Jack The Giant Killer*
(Macmillan), 1898. Signed and dated 1898. Pen and ink. 38 x 32 cm.
(SOTHEBY'S)
Illustration by Hugh Thomson (1860–1920) for *Jack The Giant Killer*
(Macmillan), 1898. Pen and ink. 38 x 32 cm.
(SOTHEBY'S)

A good example of this changing climate for children's books is shown by Rackham's contributions to the magazine *Little Folks*. Rackham produced six pictures for the 'Story of King Arthur' in 1902. They were printed in three colours, two different colours being rolled over the black of the letterpress. However, this was not sufficiently successful when the series were to be turned into book form by Cassell's, and the originals had to be reworked in full colour in 1905.

The nonsense books had been in vogue since the days of Edward Lear and were continually reprinted throughout this period. The particular flavour of the 'Nineties is well captured in Hilaire Belloc's extraordinary rhyme books published around this time. Belloc had been on holiday to Scandinavia with Lord Basil Blackwood (1870–1917) in 1891–2 and the two had amused themselves by making up verses of a more or less humorous character about the various animals that came to mind. The rhymes had that combination of nonsense and logic that so endeared itself to the Victorians, and was such a part of Lewis Carroll's legacy. The result was the publication of *The Bad Child's Book of Beasts* in 1896 with comic illustrations by 'B.T.B.', in other words, Basil Blackwood. He is a good example of the talented amateur who perfectly captures the mood of the moment. Rothenstein called him a man of great gifts, 'a little indolent perhaps — He had a turn for drawing'.[23] This book sold out of 4,000 copies in three months and has been in print ever since. It was followed by *More Beasts for Worse Children* in 1897, *The Modern Traveller* (1898), and *A Moral Alphabet* (1899), all illustrated by Blackwood. There is a great irreverence here for accepted order, the sort of thing that any child would delight in, and this mischievousness went even further in *Cautionary Tales for Children* by the same author and illustrator in 1906 and in *More Peers* as late as 1911.

It is very tempting to include Beatrix Potter's first works in this survey, but her books are really more Edwardian than Victorian in both content and colour. Miss Potter's manuscript of *Peter Rabbit* dates from well before 1900, possibly from 1893, but it was not actually published until Christmas 1901. Between 1896 and 1897 she was working on an idea that later emerged as *Squirrel Nutkin*, but that, too, did not appear until 1903. The pastel colouring of the books and the vaguely eighteenth-century scenery of some of them, for example *The Tailor of Gloucester*, make them part of the Georgian revival, dealt with in the next chapter.

Kenneth Grahame was writing for children in the 'Nineties, but his celebrated *The Wind in the Willows* (1908) was several years in the future. His *Pagan Papers* (1893) deserves to be included because of its title-page by Aubrey Beardsley and its very 'Ninety-ish Bodley Head feel. Two further books dated from this time, *The Golden Age* (1895) and *Dream Days* (1898).

CHAPTER NINE

The ILLUSTRATORS of the 'GEORGIAN' SCHOOL

In his book, *Modern Illustration* (1895), Joseph Pennell writes of the younger British artists and mentions J. Bernard Partridge as having 'fallen a victim to the eighteenth century in his striking illustrations for Mr Austin Dobson's *Beau Brocade*'.[1] Almost all the younger black-and-white artists had some dalliance with Georgian texts, illustrating in a style that came to be known as the Cranford School.

The passion for the eighteenth century began very much earlier, even if its most remarkable exponents only came to the fore in the 'Nineties. The subject matter was not typical of the *fin de siècle*, but the pen technique was definitely of its time, and the general mood of nostalgia for the *ancien régime* had its counterparts in Beardsley, Nicholson and Gordon Craig. It was really the arch-nostalgists of the mid-century, Charles Dickens, William Makepeace Thackeray and, to a lesser extent, George Augustus Sala, who had led the way. Dickens had set several of his novels in the eighteenth century, and Thackeray, an avowed admirer of Georgian art and literature, had done likewise. The fashion of the literati was for a period around 1700 which they rather vaguely called 'Queen Anne'. Thackeray fitted up a house off Kensington Square in the 'Queen Anne' style before 1860, and John Leech, the illustrator, later bought a large 'Dutch' house at The Terrace, and claimed that he 'felt like the Prince of Orange going to rest'.[2] Revivalism was in the air: society ladies like Lady Charlotte Schreiber and Lady Dorothy Nevill were collecting the artefacts of the first Georges, and architects were beginning to design suitable houses for them.

Gleeson White noticed the strong connection between books and the decorative arts. Writing of Kate Greenaway he says,

> Her gay yet 'cultured' colour, her appreciation of green chairs and formal gardens, all came at the right time. The houses by a Norman Shaw found a Morris and a Liberty ready with furniture and fabrics, and all sorts of manufacturers devoting themselves to the production of pleasant objects, to fill them; and for its drawing-room tables Miss Greenaway produced books that were in the same key.[3]

The interest in the artists of the eighteenth century was growing and was supplied by a number of books in the 1870s and 1880s. John Camden Hotten included several revived editions in his 1871 list, among them *Hood's Whims & Oddities*, *Life in London*, *The Tours of Dr Syntax* and *Cruikshank's Comic Almanacks*. John Ashton's *Chap Books of the Eighteenth Century* was also issued by Chatto & Windus in 1882.

When Thackeray published his lectures, *The Humourists of the Eighteenth Century*, in 1853 and *The Four Georges*, in 1861, he included some of his own sketches based on Georgian prints. Hogarth's graphic works, admired by Thackeray, were now of perennial interest; William Powell Frith aped them in a Victorian 'Rake's Progress' and George Augustus Sala produced a new life of the artist.[4]

In 1871, the publishers Sampson Low, Son and Marston were offering a pocket library called the Bayard series comprising 'Pleasure Books of Literature Printed in the Choicest Style'. The volumes were priced at 2*s*. 6*d*., 'printed at the Chiswick Press, bound by Burn, flexible cloth extra, gilt leaves, with silk Headbands and Registers'. The reader was offered an alternative of 'A suitable case containing 12 Volumes, price 31*s*. 6*d*.'. The series included, *The Essays of Abraham Cowley*, *Vathek* by William Beckford, *Rasselas* by Samuel Johnson, Hazlitt's *Round Table*, Lord Chesterfield's *Letters* and *The Reflections of the Duc de la Rochefoucauld*. The *Pall Mall Gazette* said, 'These little square shaped volumes contain, in a very manageable and pretty form, a great many things not very easy of access elsewhere, and some things for the first time brought together.' The series was unillustrated except for small portraits on the title-page. Although some of the Bayard titles are earlier, the majority are Georgian authors; the eighteenth century, so long reviled by tight-lipped Victorians, was starting to return.

In the late 'Eighties, Havelock Ellis was asked to become General Editor of the Mermaid series, trim pocket editions published by Vizetelly. Vizetelly seems to have lost their ownership to Fisher Unwin in 1887 and Havelock Ellis left in 1888, but a good series of Restoration and Georgian playwrights was already being produced. This cheap, attractive set was obviously intended to stir interest among a new generation. Interestingly enough, they deeply influenced Aubrey Beardsley.

Macmillan's must have been well aware of this when they began their *English Illustrated Magazine* in October 1883 under the editorship of J. Comyns Carr. Carr, and the third editor, Emery Walker, were important figures in the Arts and Crafts movement, and this fact is reflected in some very good decorations and headings in the magazine during its first ten years. Foremost among the artists was Heywood Sumner (1853–1940), whose book decorations in a woodcut style have the magical qualities of a Samuel Palmer or an Edward Calvert and yet really anticipate *art nouveau*. The leading contributors were Walter Crane, Henry Ryland, a Victorian classicist, and Alfred Parsons, the painter and designer of gardens. The enormous respect felt for the *English Illustrated* can be judged by the response of the illustrator Linley Sambourne. Writing to Mr Macmillan in early 1883 he says, 'I see you are going to start an English magazine after the style of Scribner's — If you see fit I should be proud to be put on the staff if possible.'[5] But the magazine was not all as eclectic as this suggests and one of its strengths in the 1880s was its support for eighteenth-century revivalism.

The *English Illustrated Magazine* must have pinned many of its hopes on the young and popular artist Randolph Caldecott (1846–86) who had become one of the celebrities of the *Graphic* with its big double-page Christmas spreads of life in the olden time. Caldecott touched a spring in Victorian minds by taking them back to a tranquil, agricultural world before the steam age, a world of country dances, village revels, hunting, good cheer, barons of beef and ample ale. He very skilfully created these ideal scenes, presenting his own texts in the form of narratives or picture stories. Some of his tales are given in diary or letter form, and it is not really surprising that Caldecott was, in his private life, a brilliant writer of pictorial letters.[6]

Caldecott's colour pages had the tinted tones of wash drawings and the appearance of sketch-books—'sketch-book' was a title he used effectively for some of his albums. His pages in the *Graphic*, though pitched in a story-book style, were actually read by adults who appreciated their wit and charm. In that colourful trio of Crane, Greenaway and Caldecott, he was the only one who had much of a sense of humour, or much of a talent for portraying bluff characterisations. Macmillan's had employed him, long before the *English Illustrated* was thought of, to illustrate two classics set in the late-eighteenth century, Washington Irving's *Old Christmas* (1874) and *Bracebridge Hall* (1877). The *Old Christmas* was an 'extra crown octavo', slightly larger than octavo, gilt cloth and priced at 6*s*. It had a Caldecott frontispiece, numerous pen drawings and exquisite decoration. The *Bracebridge*, though quieter, was equally elegant, with a gilt-blocked binding and decorative spine by Burn. These books were to be perfect models for many of the volumes of the 'Nineties. With decorative work for the *English Illustrated Magazine* and full-page work for the *Graphic*, it must have seemed that Caldecott's amazing talent would delight the public for years. Unhappily this was not to be the case; increasing ill health dogged him and he died in 1886, in the United States, where he was seeking a cure. His epitaphs were those two enormous folio volumes: *The Complete Collection of Pictures and Songs* (1887) and *The Complete Collection of . . . Contributions to 'The Graphic'* (1888), both published by George Routledge.

In 1886, the year of Caldecott's death, Macmillan's were extremely fortunate to acquire the full services of Hugh Thomson (1860–1920), a young draughtsman who filled this gap. Thomson was an Ulsterman who cut his teeth in the profitable Christmas card trade before coming to England to work for the *English Illustrated*. The management tested out his skills by asking him to draw an imaginary scene, 'The Parade in Bath in the last Century'. This remarkable sketch won him his commission and was the beginning of his considerable success. Thomson was an extremely skilful pen artist, his touch was light, his eye observant and he had an instinctive feeling for the past. His figures and costumes were not always scrupulously accurate, but his sense of composition was good and he always gave the public exactly what they wanted. He had clearly looked at the fine line of E. A. Abbey and combined it with the more jovial approach of Caldecott, although he never quite injected the fun of illustrating that Caldecott achieved.

Thomson's celebrity came with a technical innovation by Messrs Macmillan. In early 1886 they had decided to adopt the recently perfected process block instead of wood blocks for reproducing their line work. It was actually an economy measure because Thomson had produced so many drawings, but the artist was delighted with the results 'inasmuch as it gives to a certain extent the facsimile of my work'. As Thomas Balston wrote, 'The new process required a new art, or a new branch of art, for its sustenance. And Hugh Thomson was its pioneer'.[7] A close scrutiny of his drawing, 'Bath in the last Century', of 1884, and the drawings made by Thomson in 1886, reveal this difference. The first is beautifully worked and densely toned, the sort of drawing prepared for the wood-engravers of the 'Sixties and with difficulty interpreted by them. The later drawings are composed of uniform ink work, remarkable for the clarity of their minute detail; in short, they were drawn for that process.

This new experiment was first seen in the *English Illustrated Magazine* of April 1886, where Thomson illustrated a subject after his own heart, the second instalment of 'Days with Sir Roger de Coverley', extracted from the *Spectator* and reproduced in process. These superb pages of eighteenth-century pastiche, figures, architecture and ornament, were beautifully designed for the volume, the generous type-face doing justice to the subject. Thomson went on to illustrate more Addison, 'Coridon's Song', and poems by Isaac Walton, Henry Fielding and John Gay, in harness with the popular author Austin Dobson. The illustrator, Linley Sambourne, writing to Mr Macmillan in November 1886, commented, 'I have already congratulated Comyns Carr in the co-operation of Hugh Thomson and I now do the firm also. He is a *real* artist of the very greatest promise and there are not many about'.[8]

Thomson continued to appear frequently in the magazine, illustrating original, or supposedly original, ballads: 'A Journey to Exeter', 'Sir Dilberry Diddle' and 'Morning in London' in handsome full pages. Thomson also marked himself out as a gifted artist of contemporary life in the series 'In the Heart of London', by D. Rice Jones. Some of these sketches are nearly as good as May's, but this is not where his fame lies.

Such was the popularity of Thomson that *Days with Sir Roger de Coverley* was issued in book form in October 1886. This was a foolscap quarto edition with the illustrations on quite a large scale; Thomson's lack of training made him shy of large figure drawings.

In 1890, Macmillan's began a series, known after 1893 as the 'Cranford' series although *Cranford* was not the first book in the line. The name stuck and has been given since the 1930s to the 'Cranford' School of illustrators, a description which is neither comprehensive nor accurate to describe the eighteenth-century revival. The books were crown octavo volumes in green cloth with gold blocking, a conscious revival of *Old Christmas* of thirteen years earlier, but also a studied exercise in showing off Hugh Thomson's dexterity. They began with *The Vicar of Wakefield* for the Christmas market of 1890. Thomson's terms for the job were probably five pounds for full pages, three pounds for half pages, two pounds for decorative tailpieces, the amounts he received for the *Cranford* volume of 1891.[9] Immediately the success of the Goldsmith was realised, Kegan Paul offered Thomson £150 to illustrate *The Ballad of Beau Brocade* by Austin Dobson, thus starting a rivalry, and also a whole series of 'Cranford' look-alikes that have confused booksellers, collectors and librarians ever since.

In 1894 the publisher, George Allen, enlisted Thomson to illustrate Jane Austen's *Pride and Prejudice*, a brilliant choice, which Macmillan's must have

'Morning in London' by Hugh Thomson (1860–1920) for the *English Illustrated Magazine*, 1887.

wished they had first thought of. This charming production looks precisely like the 'Cranford' books, and its appearance shook the original publisher and the artist. To counter this, Macmillan's at once commissioned Thomson, on 1 December, 1893, to illustrate the remaining Jane Austen novels, *Emma, Mansfield Park, Northanger Abbey, Persuasion, Sense and Sensibility* and *Lady Susan*. Thomson evidently thought his old employers could buy back the rights of *Pride and Prejudice* from George Allen at the same time. 'I regret extremely', he wrote to Macmillan on 18 March, 1894, 'the impression which I seem to have given Mr George Macmillan that you intended making Mr Allen an offer for the "Pride and Prejudice" drawings. I never had any impression of that kind. When I said to Mr Macmillan that you might buy them, it was an opinion, wrongly and carelessly expressed, which I have had that if the book was offered on reasonable terms you

'The warm west-looking window-seat' by Hugh Thomson (1860–
1920) for *The Ballad of Beau Brocade* by Austin Dobson, 1892.

might take it over . . . My unfortunate tongue which never expresses what
I want to say, always gets me into hot water.'[10] This does explain how much
of a rage the eighteenth-century style had become in the early 'Nineties.

The new series that had arisen from this cut-throat competition was
called 'Macmillan's Illustrated Standard Novels' (1895 to 1901); it included
the Austen novels and eventually ran to forty titles. To my mind this is a
far less attractive series in every way; bound in red with blind decoration
and the title in gold, the books have few frills, although the illustrations
are excellent. This series in turn spawned other rivals: Service and Paton's

Illustration by Hugh Thomson (1860–1920) for *Scenes of Clerical Life* by George Eliot, 1906. Signed and dated 1905. Pen and ink.
(MAAS GALLERY)

'Illustrated English Library' and Bliss, Sands & Co.'s 'Illustrated Standard Novels'. The last successful imitations were Dent's 'Essay Series' after 1900. Such excitement generated a great deal of high-class pen-and-ink work for the younger illustrators. Hugh Thomson remained their leader, but the 'Cranford' School included several artists who outstripped him in actual talent and whose interests were more varied.

The increasing interest in colour in the 'Nineties had its effect and the original *Cranford* volume was issued with forty coloured plates in October 1896 for the Christmas market of that year. Artists were concerned at losing control of their familiar black-and-white world and Thomson wrote anxiously to his publishers, 'I need scarcely say that I should prefer that the 'Cranford' cuts should be coloured by me rather than anyone else and I am obliged to you for giving me the refusal of the work'.[11]

Hugh Thomson's second career was to be in these illustrated Edwardian gift-books. The transition from the black-and-white work of the 'Nineties to the scintillating colour of the 1900s, where Rackham and Dulac were supreme, was difficult; the technological revolution was almost as dramatic as the change from the silents to the talkies. Some of the great illustrators were never to achieve it, but Thomson's deft pen line combined with pastel colouring gave him a smooth transition. The dazzling gift-books began with George Eliot's *Scenes of Clerical Life* (1906), *As You Like It* (1909), *The Merry Wives of Windsor* (1910), *The School for Scandal* (1911), *She Stoops to Conquer* (1912) and J. M. Barrie's *Quality Street* (1913). This formidable collection was brought to a halt by the First World War.

When Thomson's fourth title in the 'Cranford' series, *Our Village* by Miss Mitford, appeared in 1893, it was accompanied by another book, *Hood's Humorous Poems*, illustrated by Charles Brock. C. E. Brock (1870–1938) was the first of a whole group of Thomson followers who were to have success in the 'Nineties and in the years following. C. E., and his brother, H. M. Brock (1875–1960) lived a quiet, almost cloistered, existence in Cambridge, picturing the world of Jane Austen, Charles Lamb,

Illustration by C. E. Brock (1870–1938) for *Humorous Poems* by
Thomas Hood (Macmillan), 1893. Signed and dated 1893. Pen and
ink.
(SOTHEBY'S)

168

'Queen Mab' by C. E. Brock (1870–1938) for *Humorous Poems* by
Thomas Hood (Macmillan), 1893.

Oliver Goldsmith and Daniel Defoe. C.E.'s illustrations to *Humorous Poems*
are delicately fresh; they have a finer line than some of Thomson's work,
and a greater humour and aptitude for the figure. In some of the headings
and initial letters there is a real link with the more robust world of Caldecott, and the imaginative scope of Richard Doyle. The Brocks were
extremely anxious to add accuracy to their other talents, and kept a stock
of costume and furniture for the same reason that Thomson had portfolios
of old engravings. All the same, the dresses have an obstinate "ninety-ish"
feel and the dates are sometimes mixed. C. E. Brock, who I think is the
more interesting artist of the two, went on to illustrate *Gulliver's Travels*
(1894), *Pride and Prejudice* (as a direct challenge to George Allen) and *Annals
of the Parish* in 1895, and Fennimore Cooper's *The Pathfinder* in 1900. For
'The English Illustrated Library' he did an edition of *Ivanhoe* (1897) and
The Vicar of Wakefield (1898). Brock's value to the series was considerable,
but at the end of 1894, while working on both *The Annals of the Parish* and
Pride and Prejudice and being badgered by Macmillan's for drawings for
Kingsley, he protested. Writing to Macmillan he said, 'I might mention
that I have had to refuse several very good offers, including one of more
than £4 a drawing, and as I know that 'Westward Ho' if I am to do it, will
want a lot of time and research, I should be very pleased if you could see
your way to increasing the remuneration you offer'.[12]

H. M. Brock's career proper began in 1895, when he drew spirited
drawings for a Marryat novel, and later for titles by Samuel Lover and
Fennimore Cooper in 1896 and 1900. He was to illustrate yet another
edition of *Cranford* for 'The English Illustrated Library' in 1898. The
younger Brock married the sister of Fred Pegram (1870–1937), another
'Cranford' artist who illustrated Disraeli's *Sybil* for Macmillan in 1895.

'An old butler' by F. H. Townsend (1868–1920) for *Maid Marian and Crotchet Castle* by T. L. Peacock (Macmillan), 1895.

F. H. Townsend (1868–1920), who is now remembered as a *Punch* cartoonist and the magazine's first art editor, was a very active illustrator in the 1890s. He was strongly influenced by the master draughtsman, E. A. Abbey, and falls naturally into the 'Georgian' School for which he made some superb drawings. These include several books with the obligatory eighteenth or early nineteenth-century *mise-en-scène*: the Peacock novels, *Maid Marian and Crotchet Castle* (1895), *Gryll Grange* and *Melincourt* (1896), *The Misfortunes of Elphin* (1896), Captain Marryat's *The Kings Own* (1897) and two Brontë titles, *Jane Eyre* and *Shirley* (1897). Townsend's drawings for *Crotchet Castle* are very accomplished, particularly since there is little action to illustrate and the humour is in the philosophical dialogue. Such sketches as 'An Old Butler' have rather more substance than similar pages by the Brocks.

We have already met J. Bernard Partridge as the illustrator of Anstey's light-hearted stories, but he was also a brilliant designer in this genre. The best examples are his captivating drawings for *Proverbs in Porcelain* by Austin Dobson, produced as a 'Cranford' rival by Kegan Paul in 1893. Sentimental they may be, but Partridge's pen illustrations are full of vitality, 'brilliant dash'[13] and period flavour. His care and attention to detail,

Title-page by Bernard Partridge (1861–1945) for *Proverbs in Porcelain* by Austin Dobson (Kegan Paul), 1893.

and the gradations of hatching, bring out the folds and textures of the ample costumes. His later cartoon work was to strip him of this delicacy, and presumably of the strong decorative sense which is apparent on every page, specially in the headings. It is worth remembering that the veteran German artist, Adolph Menzel, spoke admiringly of Partridge's work when William Rothenstein met him in 1900.

Other 'Georgian' illustrators were H. R. Millar, the Hammond sisters and E. J. Sullivan. Harold R. Millar (1869–1940) was a student of the Birmingham School, but did not retain its tight-knit style. On the contrary, he developed a very broad and free kind of pen work, which could be darkly toned at one point and finely drawn at another, lending great drama to his pages. He appears here as the illustrator of Peacock's *Headlong Hall* and *Nightmare Abbey* (1896), going on to draw for Captain Marryat's works in 1896–7. Millar had already made a slight reputation as a portrayer of eastern subjects; he collected and studied oriental weapons and so was ideal for James Morier's *The Adventures of Hajji Baba* (1895). He was also excellent for *The Silver Fairy Book*, being a good illustrator of children's stories; James Thorpe particularly enthused over his work for E. Nesbit's tales: 'These showed excellent fancy, were well drawn and generally contained a cunningly placed and effective patch of black.'[14]

Miss Chris Hammond (1861–1900) illustrated several books for the 'Cranford' series. They were *Castle Rackrent*, *The Absentee*, *Popular Tales*, *Helen*, *Belinda*, and *The Parents' Assistant*, all written by Maria Edgeworth and all published in 1895. She continued these period settings for 'The Illustrated English Library' with Thackeray's *Henry Esmond*, *Pendennis* and *Vanity Fair* in 1897, and, in 1898, *The Newcomes* and Lytton's *The Caxtons* for good measure. She had a delicate and competent pen style and could turn her hand to almost any magazine or novel illustrating. Considering that she was not yet forty when she died, her output was considerable. It included work for most of the better commercial journals of the 'Nineties. Gertrude Demain Hammond (1860–1952), her sister, followed Chris into period illustration. Her work included *Goldsmith's Comedies* (1894–5), *The Virginians* by W. M. Thackeray (1902), and a number of Edwardian giftbooks; she also makes an appearance in *The Yellow Book*.

The one artist who stands quite alone in this group, and whose stature is greater than any of them, is E. J. Sullivan (1869–1933). He is included here because he contributed *The School for Scandal* and *Tom Brown's School Days* (1896) to the 'Cranford' series, and illustrated a number of other books with eighteenth-century or period settings. Edmund Joseph Sullivan was born in London, the son of an artist, and served his apprenticeship at the recently founded *Daily Graphic*. He developed into an illustrator whose imagination and breadth of mind made him the equal of any of his contemporaries with the exception of Beardsley and Ricketts. His great vigour as a draughtsman was combined with an amazing facility to illustrate abstract subjects from literature in a new and convincing way. For this reason he was often engaged to draw for very difficult, semi-philosophical books, such as the writings of Thomas Carlyle which needed an intellectual capacity and a wit rather above the normal. Sullivan was an extremely gifted teacher, as a lecturer on book illustration and design at Goldsmith's College, and he wrote two important textbooks on his art, *Line: An Art Study* (1921) and *The Art of Illustration* (1922). They are noted for their insights into the key figures of early twentieth-century illustration and their perceptive look at techniques.

Apart from the Sheridan and Hughes titles already mentioned, Sullivan illustrated *Lavengro* by George Borrow for 'Macmillan's Illustrated Standard Novels' in 1896. Borrow's vivid but rambling text is hard to augment by drawings, and Sullivan has exercised considerable discipline in concentrating on linked incidents or characters, to gather together extremely long runs of text. Sullivan's original sketch-book for this early volume demonstrates how carefully he has read the text and extracted its most visual episodes. These are laid out in sequence in rapid pencil, and developed in ink in places where a particular image has struck him as important. There is actually not a great deal of alteration between these rough drafts and the incisive black-and-white illustrations in the book. According to Percy V. Bradshaw, there were at least two intermediary stages, one to form the composition and one to set the drawing on stiff card the same size as the illustration.[15] Sullivan's intention, worked out in this book, was to create a dramatic impression by intensely finished lines in one part of the drawing, leaving the background or landscape quite sketchy. Although the book is variable in quality, the blame may be laid at the door of the publisher for the unattractive binding, the ordinary paper and the lack of decoration in what was a very commercial series.

Sullivan was a more full-bodied draughtsman than any of this School, and in such superb illustrations as the pump scene in *Lavengro*, he shows his enormous debt to Pinwell and the 'Sixties artists. But curiously enough he did not transfer well to the coloured gift-book; there was something too robust and masculine in his handling. He brought out a further *Lavengro* in 1914 with twelve colour plates, to match a coloured *The Vicar of Wakefield* of the same year, but these were not successes.

In 1898 the artist produced a small masterpiece, Thomas Carlyle's *Sartor Resartus*, for George Bell & Sons. The seventy-nine line drawings, and also the over-all design of pages, cover and spine, are exceptional, making Sullivan one of the most skilled, thoughtful illustrators of the 'Nineties. Sullivan wrote of it, 'I addressed myself to the undertaking because I saw in it an opportunity to make drawings almost entirely for their own sake, as a holiday from the conditions that so often bind the modern artist to the pettiness and trivialities of the moment'.[16]

Thorpe quite rightly suggests that Sullivan has 'mimicked' the German accent of Carlyle's book by illustrating the text in a teutonic way with overtones of Dürer, the German engravers and Menzel. A more potent influence, surely, would be the work of the contemporary illustrator, Joseph Sattler (1867–1931), whose extraordinary illustrated volumes, *Gershicte der rheinischen Stadtzkultur* and *Durcheinarder*, were published in Berlin in 1897. There is a bite and a ferocity in these German works which certainly find echoes in Sullivan, but, more revealingly, there are chapter headings in the *Durcheinarder* which could well be Sullivan's for *Sartor Resartus*! Charles Hiatt had written an article on Sattler for the *Studio* as early as 1894, in Sullivan's most impressionable period, but the artist makes no reference to the German in either of his textbooks. Hiatt published Sattler's 'Modern Dance of Death',[17] which had been exhibited at the Salon, and the *Sartor Resartus* illustrations bear many similarities to it. Sullivan mixes sign and symbol in a most effective way, the illustrations ranging from the patterned and the complex to the disarmingly simple, from the strange and striking 'Herr Diogenes' to the seductive pose of 'Blumine'. Sullivan's genius as a decorator is apparent in the diversity of the initial letters and headings, although one feels that a book of more generous proportions would have revealed his talents.[18]

In 1900 he had the opportunity to serve another great Victorian, Alfred, Lord Tennyson, when he illustrated *A Dream of Fair Women* for Grant Richards. The large paper edition of this book certainly gave him full scope for page-illustrating and the result is a lovely volume of handsome images. A contemporary wrote that 'his drawings are always something more than mere Illustrations — they are illuminating interpretations of an author's thoughts'.[19] Given that *The Dream* is an early and untypical work, Sullivan releases in his designs of the fair ones a liveliness and variety which the

'Herr Diogenes' by E. J. Sullivan (1869–1933) for *Sartor Resartus* by Thomas Carlyle (George Bell), 1898.

'The Departure' by E. J. Sullivan (1869–1933) for *A Dream of Fair Women* by Lord Tennyson (Grant Richards), 1900.

'The Day Dream' by E. J. Sullivan (1869–1933) for *A Dream of Fair Women* by Lord Tennyson (Grant Richards), 1900.

text might have made cloying. He is never interested in prettiness, and it is actually in the more imaginative side of the book, such as in 'The Vision of Sin' and 'The Palace of Art', that his powers are most extended. These drawings are very far from the costume fancies of a Thomson or a Brock and are totally representative of the *fin de siècle*.

Two of Sullivan's later books were also in this cerebral vein which suited him best: the sturdy *Pilgrim's Progress* (1901) and Goldsmith's *A Citizen of the World* (1904). Works by Burns, Gilbert White and Le Motte Fouqué kept him busy in the mid-1900s, leading up to his magnificent two-volume edition of Carlyle's *The French Revolution* (1910). This is in the format of an Edwardian gift-book but happily its illustrations are confined to black-and-white. Sullivan's genius for using symbols is well displayed in the book; this is a response perhaps to the great visual tradition of the Georgian political print and caricature (though his figures are never caricatured). 'You look in vain', Bradshaw wrote, 'in these Illustrations, for realistic or repulsive crowds shrieking for the blood of the aristocracy. The realist has to be content with admirably drawn, but very free pen and ink portraits of the principal characters. For the big episodes, Sullivan has looked beyond the incident which would provide an "effective subject", and has represented symbolically the cause which produced the incident.'[19]

'The Vision of Sin' by E. J. Sullivan (1869–1933) for *A Dream of Fair Women* by Lord Tennyson (Grant Richards), 1900.

Sullivan's later work included the rather savagely patriotic *The Kaiser's Garland* (1915) and *Maud* (1922), a slim volume with coloured or tinted plates, which somehow prejudice the intuitive 'colour' in his black-and-white work. By 1922 this would have appeared very Victorian. Gordon Ray was probably correct to term him 'a belated Victorian', but he was a very great one indeed.[20]

At the time that Hugh Thomson was beginning to establish himself in the pages of the *English Illustrated Magazine*, another artist was also prominent there. This was Herbert Railton (1857–1910), who had a penchant for depicting old buildings, and endowing them with a sort of patina of age and mystery. Macmillan's had the extremely bright idea that Thomson's figures might be put together with Railton's crumbling architecture to form a book. Since there was still much interest in the history of the road — the coaching revival really dated from the 'Seventies — the two artists were commissioned to illustrate W. Outram Tristram's *Coaching Days and Coaching Ways* which appeared in 1888, with smaller editions in later years. Railton's nervous pen lines, depicting the odd corners of inn yards, forgotten bridges and turnpikes, and the half-hidden frontage of a manor house contained in a feigned border, were extremely decorative. They matched well the groups of ostlers and dairy-maids that Thomson loved to draw. Railton's pupil, Holland Tringham (d.1909) did the same sort of work and these two must be given some credit for starting all those picturesque guides of the 1900s in which highways and byways were tinged with nostalgia. Railton's work, though topographical, is as much a part of the Georgian revival as any of the 'Cranford' illustrators.

Cecil Aldin (1870–1935) gained most popularity after the turn of the century, but he is certainly a member of this group, having illustrated

'La Fille Aux Yeux D'Or' by Charles Conder (1868–1909), 1898.
Ink and watercolour. 22.4 × 15.8 cm.
(CECIL HIGGINS ART GALLERY, BEDFORD)

W. M. Praed's *Everyday Characters* (1896). Aldin was trained at Frank Calderon's 'Animal' Art School and so his depiction of horses, dogs and horse-drawn conveyances is splendidly accurate. He had early drawings published in the *English Illustrated Magazine* and in the *Graphic* as early as 1891. His real success came with *Two Well-Worn Shoes* (1899), *The Fallowfield Hunt* (1899–1900) and *Dog Days* (1902).

With the exception of Sullivan, none of these eighteenth-century-inspired draughtsman could be called particularly original in their ideas, but that is certainly not true of the painter and occasional illustrator Charles Conder (1868–1909). He was a painter-muralist and a designer of rather exotic decoration, a product of the Paris of the 'Eighties and 'Nineties, and the circle of painters who frequented Montmartre. The fragility of his work — scenes of poetic imagination and beautiful colours on silks — was mirrored by a fragility of personality; Conder was a confirmed alchoholic, a great womaniser and incapable of managing his own affairs. William Rothenstein credits him with being an early devotee of the eighteenth century. 'To say that he belonged more to the eighteenth century than to his own, is too obvious. His art was based partly on his own sense of style, of gesture, of artificial comedy, in a word, the comedy of Davenant, of Congreve, and of Watteau and Fragonard . . .'[21] Rothenstein felt that Conder's influence on Beardsley was marked. 'The inspiration of Morris and Burne-Jones was waning fast,' he wrote of the 1894 period, 'and the eighteenth-century illustrators were taking the place of the Japanese print.'[22]

After Beardsley's dismissal by Lane and his adoption by Leonard Smithers for *The Savoy*, Smithers, who became a baleful influence on Beardsley, acquired the services of Conder as well. He asked Conder to illustrate a favourite Balzac story, *La Fille aux Yeux d'Or*. Rothenstein mentions that Conder was particularly keen on designing book covers and the Balzac provided him with an opportunity to experiment. 'I persuaded him, too, to try lithography — his pencil drawings had the quality of lithographs — and he made a number of admirable drawings, mostly illustrating Balzac, on transfer paper.'[23]

Smithers encouraged Conder's drinking excesses which brought on an attack of *delirium tremens*, greatly alarming Rothenstein. Conder fortunately escaped to Dieppe where he completed the Balzac illustrations. The finished drawing shown here is very free, a set of cameo illustrations set in a decorative border with supporting figures, a title-page with the melancholy of Watteau about it.

Conder contributed another eighteenth-century watercolour to the *Pageant* (1896) entitled 'L'Oiseau Bleu', but his pictures were always more inspirations from texts than literal interpretations of them.

CHAPTER TEN

The END of an EPOCH

'The old world was passing and I found myself looking out a little anxiously for the New Jerusalem descending from above. I never saw it, and what's more I haven't seen it yet.'
W. GRAHAM ROBERTSON

The fact that the 'Nineties was a period which respected and enthused over book design, was reflected in many minor aspects of art printing. A decade that admired the work of Whistler, the 'Butterfly' of so many brilliant prints and verbal quips, also took to its heart the ephemera of the art world. The book, whether the product of a private press like The Vale or the latest in a beautifully fashioned series like the 'Cranford', was an object of decorative art in its own right, to be opened with veneration by the collector. The 'collector' rather than the 'reader' might be the correct appellation in the 'Nineties, because the volumes of the *fin de siècle* were rated increasingly in the *Studio* and elsewhere for the illustrations rather than the text. The true bibliophile would not write his or her name in the book, but would insert a specially designed book-plate; this would not only denote the ownership, but also enhance the beauty of the book.

The pictorial book-plate enjoyed something of a revival in the 'Nineties. That elderly aesthete, Lord de Tabley, had prepared the way by publishing his *Guide to the Study of Bookplates* (1880, republished in 1900). A succession of books followed and the Ex Libris Society was founded in 1891, but a fresh impetus must have been provided by the attention given to book-plates in the *Studio*, and to their practical value within the Arts and Crafts movement. The book-plate was undoubtedly the simplest and most personal piece of art patronage that the ordinary person could indulge in. Here, in the art-conscious 'Nineties, was the perfect way to express the persona and enable oneself or some other artist to create an original design! The craze, for that is what it became, mushroomed to book-plate collecting and was severely criticised by Gleeson White.

'Rubbish, be it in the form of book-plates or cigar ends, is merely rubbish, and charms you no more after it has been sorted, classified, collected, and indexed, than when it reposed in the waste-paper basket, or lay unheeded in the gutter.'[1] White was critical of the book-plates or labels that were larger than they should be and of ones that were simply a picture without any reference to purpose.

> It is surely not asking too much of a book-plate that it should betray both idea and adequate execution. Possibly, if either the idea or its rendering is surprisingly good, one may forgive the absence of the other quality; but when both idea and execution are tame and foolish, when neither symbolism nor decoration are more than trite and hackneyed, when the whole design has but one dominant note, and that is 'arrant vulgarity,' both in idea and execution, strong words are needful, and unless the book-plate is to become contemptible, some of its admirers should come forward to purge their collections of unworthy specimens.[2]

White was particularly critical of the English Ex Libris Society whose influence he considered 'positively harmful' to design.[3] He was not principally concerned with heraldic book-plates here but with those which were based on modern styles and idioms, and mirrored a branch, if a minor branch, of book illustration itself.

Many of the major book illustrators that we have looked at designed one or two plates for their friends; others made many more, in effect becoming specialists in the field. Walter Crane designed one for Clement Shorter, signed with the well-known 'bottle and crane' in the corner, and E. A. Abbey designed one for himself and for several others. J. J. Guthrie produced a number of designs, some incorporating a scheme of white on black, which were more labels than plates, and added some powerful figure work to his series. Paul Woodroffe and Charles Robinson both made book-plates, the latter for the art teacher, Fred Brown. Laurence Housman made only a few plates, a paucity which Gleeson White deplored: 'Why more people do not endeavour to secure designs by Mr Housman (cut on wood if possible, by his sister) is a mystery. Perhaps he declines commissions, for there seems to be no other logical reason for that most ingenious and accomplished draughtsman being represented by such a small number of book-plates . . .'[4]

He considered the Birmingham-trained E. H. New to be exceptional in his use of alphabets, a difficult discipline. He also admired the most celebrated book-plates from William Nicholson's hand, his 'Phil May' of 1895 and his Heinemann 'Windmill'. White called them 'typical of his method'.[5]

E. Gordon Craig, as we have seen, made a business out of producing book-plates, silhouetted galleons for James Pryde, tiny painted fleur-de-lis for himself. 'It would seem', wrote White, 'that Mr Gordon Craig almost alone among modern designers, has recognised that a simple device is more suitable than an elaborate design.'[6] Younger artists such as A. Garth Jones, Celia Levetus and Alan Wright worked on book-plates although their output was not prolific. A few artists, like the heraldic designer, Harold Nelson, were actually specialists in this area. Henry Ospovat, too, was apparently intending to follow the same path: 'Knowing the artistic sympathies of the artist, and the painstaking attention he bestows upon every subject, it is impossible not to believe that he will soon be reckoned among the best of the few designers who lay themselves out to design *ex libris*.'[7]

One would expect Aubrey Beardsley to have made an important contribution to this minor art, but this is not the case. He designed only four authenticated book-plates besides one for himself. White comments acidly:

Book-plate by Charles Robinson (1870–1937). Published in the
Studio, 1898.

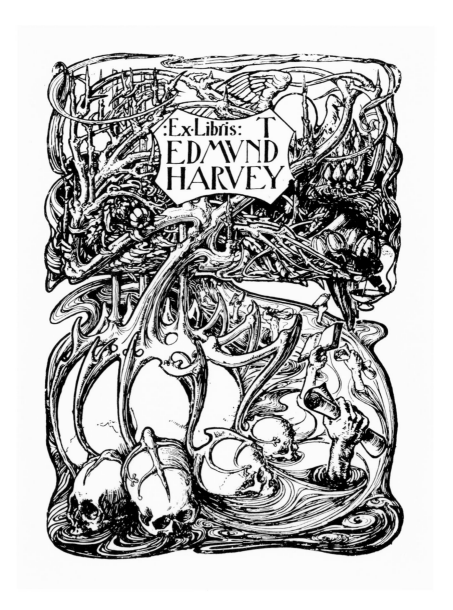

Book-plate by Cyril Goldie (1872–1942). Published in the *Studio*, 1898.

'That the latter could ever be used, except in "top-shelf" volumes, is doubtful, it is an unhappy instance of the perverted fancy which the greatest admirers of the genius of the wonderful black-and-white artist can but regret.'

Gleeson White himself designed a book-plate for his daughter,[8] as did Aymer Vallance, the writer, for his. The majority of such designs caught the spirit of the age, whether they were in the late Pre-Raphaelite style, or the Renaissance manner of Ricketts and Shannon, with the design all hung about with trophies of the owner's interests, or whether they were the chunky, direct woodcuts of Craig and Nicholson. They proclaim very forcibly that the *fin de siècle* was a time when the printed page mattered and when owners of libraries, however small, were proud of their possessions.

The Christmas card industry was booming during our period; the Vic-

Book-plates by Aubrey Beardsley (1872–98) and Robert Anning
Bell (1863–1933). Both published in *The Yellow Book*, Vol. 1, April
1894.

torian's love of seasonal sentiment, fostered by 'art' and rapid communication, made the Christmas card immensely popular. Kate Greenaway had
been an industrious producer of cards in the 1870s; in fact she was a
discovery of the firm of Marcus Ward which pursued a policy of producing
high-quality 'aesthetic' cards. Other artists belonging to Marcus Ward
were Walter Crane, Miss A. M. Lockyer, Henry Rylands and Moyr Smith.
Later, Hugh Thomson was to be one of the firm's stars although their lack
of recognition of his book illustrating talents resulted in his resignation. A
generation of artists grew up who, in the 1880s, were primarily Christmas
card designers, artists such as W. S. Coleman (nubile young girls on
rocks) and Alice Havers (Albert Moore ladies on balconies) who produced
substitutes for anything truly inventive. The fashion in the 1890s was for
Christmas card companies to fasten onto popular pictures in the Summer
Exhibition of the Royal Academy and to have cards made from them,
rather than commission original designs.[9]

Gleeson White felt that this was a sad falling off from earlier days:
'. . . buyers today appear to be content to accept prettiness as the equival-
ent of beauty — or, in other cases, to rush to the other extreme, and accept
grotesque originality as the highest beauty. That Aubrey Beardsley, Mr

R. Anning Bell and other distinguished artists, have not (so far as I know) been asked to design a card, shows in itself that the industry is content to fall behind the taste of the moment, be it good or evil.'[10]

In fact the best cards produced during the 'Nineties were not those of the commercial firms at all, but 'private cards' designed by the artists themselves for their family and friends. Gleeson White published a few of these admirable examples in the *Studio* article. Because of the cost of colour, they were usually in black and white, no great disadvantage to Birmingham artists such as C. M. Gere, Georgie Cave France and Sidney Heath, whose preferred way of working this was. These Arts and Crafts card makers tend to go for religious or seasonal themes more readily than the commercial companies. Some, such as those by Alice Woodward and E. H. New, with careful delineation and script and flowing 'Morrisy' borders, are perfect evocations of their age.

This minute attention to every aspect of design was typical of the period, and also typical of those figures like White, Vallance and Lane who were fastidious about their designers' work. A very important man, but a shadowy figure of the 'Nineties was Charles Holme of the *Studio*, influential beyond his character, but clearly a man of parts. No biography exists of Holme, as it does of Lane and Ross, and one's impressions are gained from the comments of those who knew him. An early colleague was Walter Shaw Sparrow, assistant art editor of the *Studio* in the crucial years 1899–1904. Sparrow was at the very heart of this arts revival and yet wrote rather equivocally of it in later years:

> In the nineties, let me remind you, a varied style came into vogue known as *Art Nouveau*. Its diversity of appeal was very wide, ranging from Brangwyn carpets and chairs to Voysey cretonnes, wall-papers, houses, carpets, cottages, and furniture; and from posters by Cheret, Grasset, Willette, Casier, Privat-Livermont, and many others, to black-and-white drawings ornamented with patterns of graceful curves and flourishes. Historians have begun to look back upon *Art Nouveau* with more pleasure than the British people got from its adventures; for its pioneering had in it many good things. Like the Morris movement, it was too fond of pattern — pattern everywhere; but the patterning, in many cases, was original, and not an adaptation from old models of style. Many persons believed that Holme was too friendly towards certain phases of *Art Nouveau*, and also to Beardsley, whose unique and unearthly genius influenced too many young designers.[11]

If this is unfair on Beardsley, it is certainly true that the reverberations of the 'Nineties were to echo down the years, both in the *Studio* and in other publications. Because the *fin de siècle* was the second golden age of book illustration, perhaps the silver age, its influences were to leave an indelible impression on teaching. Within a dozen years there were three art schools, privately run, largely devoted to the teaching of book illustration. John Hassall's successful venture at Stratford Studios was founded soon after 1900, and the Byam Shaw School was founded off Kensington Church Street in 1910, shortly to be followed by Percy V. Bradshaw's The Press Art School at Tudor Hall, Forest Hill. All this would have been utterly unthinkable before the 1890s.

With a strange and tragic irony, the end of the 'Nineties was also the end for so many gifted and inventive illustrators. The toll of talent was remorseless: Aubrey Beardsley died in 1898, James McNeill Whistler in 1903, Phil May in 1904, Charles Conder in 1909, and there were many more. The leaders of aestheticism were also making their final curtain calls: Walter Pater in 1894, Oscar Wilde in 1900, Henry Harland in 1905. Among the more Olympian figures of an earlier generation, the 'Nineties witnessed the deaths of Lord Leighton, J. E. Millais, William Morris and Burne-Jones.

Some distinguished artists had an 'Indian summer' of work and activity in these years, notably George Louis Palmella Busson du Maurier (1834–96). George du Maurier had had a remarkable career with *Punch*, becoming a master of the social subject and inventing a whole cast of typically Victorian characters. In the early days he had done much serious illustration of fiction and in some ways his *Punch* work was more factual than directly humorous. It is still a quarry of period detail, from the hang of dresses to the taste for Japanese fans. Below the surface, du Maurier nurtured a desire for greater fame and the wish to be taken as a literary man in his own right. Frustrated ambitions to write dated back to his friendship with Thackeray in the days of the *Cornhill Magazine*, but it was only in the 'Nineties that these ambitions were realised.

By 1890, du Maurier's *Punch* work was tedious to him and he was hampered by increasingly poor eyesight; he had lost an eye while still a student, (a disability, incidentally, shared by Tenniel). To overcome this trouble he created his drawings on a larger scale, but could hardly disguise his boredom with the work. The subject matter becomes more and more stereotyped and the *causes célèbres* of the time, the advent of *art nouveau*, the Beardsley boom and the Arts and Crafts movement, are not even satirised. Du Maurier was putting all his efforts into literary work, which resulted in three remarkable novels in these closing years of his life.

The germ of an idea for a story about his student life in Paris had long lain dormant. Du Maurier was an instinctive autobiographer and a good descriptive writer, but he had no experience in putting together a sustained narrative or developing a rounded character. His first novel, *Peter Ibbetson*, published in *Harper's Monthly* in 1891, met with a moderate success. The hero, an idealised portrait of himself, has the same Anglo-French background and is brought up in similar surroundings in Paris and London. The descriptions of childhood are among the best things du Maurier ever wrote and Peter Ibbetson's unrequited love for a childhood sweetheart, now out of his reach, seems a simple enough theme. But du Maurier complicates this by bringing the lovers together in dreams, a device worthy of Poe and guaranteed to capture a 'Nineties audience. He had not intended to pepper his novel with sketches, but the poet, William Allingham, thought this essential,[12] as did the eventual publisher of the book, Osgood McIlvaine. The artist designed some vignette illustrations and a few full-page ones for his book, most of them spirited and effective, although the transition from the 1840s to the 1880s is made with difficulty. Neither the style of the drawings nor the design of the book are at all typical of the 'Nineties —there is a lack of decoration on the pages and the blue cover with gold blocking looks back to the 'Eighties. But the contents, with a thin dividing line between the real and unreal, a concern with the supernatural and a hankering after a glorious past, had aspects much loved by 'Nineties readers.

'A Voice He didn't Understand.' by George du Maurier (1834–96)
for *Trilby*, 1895.

Du Maurier's second novel was *Trilby*, published in *Harper's Magazine* in 1894 and in book form in 1895. It was a runaway bestseller and exactly the book the author had hoped for. The story of a Parisian *grisette*, loved by an English artist and mesmerised by an evil foreigner who destroys her, is more powerful in both text and illustration than his previous work. Du Maurier based it on his own experiences in Paris once again, but also on Henri Murger's *Scènes de la Vie de Bohème*, published in 1845. As a memory of student life and a portrait of an innocent artist's model, in Trilby herself, the book is excellent, and the developing genius of the evil Svengali is well handled. The second part of the book is less convincing. The illustrations are of a higher standard; some of the vignettes and decorative drawings, such as a marvellous view of the Champs Elysées, are pure 'Nineties work, as are the scenes of carriages and hansom cabs. Some of the figure studies of drunks and bohemians, too, are on a par with Keene or May.

The fact that du Maurier based his story on real life was dangerous. His characters were easily identifiable as living people, no longer carefree and reckless students, but distinguished academicians and leaders of taste. The book contained pen portraits of the artists Edward Poynter, Tom Armstrong and Stacy Marks, but much more seriously, in 'Joe Sibley', a pen portrait and a pen likeness of Whistler! 'Always in debt, like Svengali; like Svengali, vain, witty, and a most exquisite and original artist; and also eccentric in his attire (though clean), so that people would stare at him as he walked along—which he adored!'[13] Whistler, who was something of a vexatious litigant, immediately sprang to the attack, threatened to take *Harper's* to law, insisted that du Maurier should resign from two clubs and wrote letters to the papers. The result was an alteration in the book version, du Maurier having to expunge the laughable character of Sibley, although it could not be changed in the first version.

Du Maurier, by now elderly and exhausted, tried to repeat the success of *Trilby* in another novel, *The Martian*, published in 1896 after his death. This was also autobiographical, the two leading characters Josselin and Maurice being two sides of du Maurier's complex nature. He had also illustrated this book, but with less conviction than in the earlier volumes. It was yet another version of the *fin de siècle* tragic enigma; success cheated one by coming too late, as death cheated others by coming too early.

They knelt on the divan, with their elbows on the window-sill, and watched the street-lamps popping into life along the quays —and looked out through the gathering dusk for

Vignette illustration by George du Maurier (1834–96) for *Trilby*, 1895.

If one were looking for a Valhalla of the 'Nineties, one would turn instinctively to the work of the caricaturists. This would not be found in *Punch*, then enjoying one of its periods of comatose complacency, or even in the commercial press, but in the little magazines we have already considered. There, at intervals, appeared the exquisite talents of Max Beerbohm (1872–1956), capturing in a few lines the essence of the age.

Beerbohm's career as a caricaturist began rather tentatively at Merton College, Oxford and later in the *Strand Magazine* with 'Club Types' (September to December 1892) and 'Oxford at Home' (January 1895). He was later to describe this last commission as 'a great moment'.[14] Max was an avowed admirer of the *portrait chargé* style, a Continental development where the portrait study was exaggerated rather than caricatured. This perfectly suited the Victorian psyche where savagery was taboo but an irreverent satire was acceptable. The great practioner of the style was 'Ape' or Carlo Pellegrini (1838–89), who had practically guaranteed the success of the magazine *Vanity Fair* with his witty diminutive plates. A number of artists followed in his footsteps including Walter Sickert (1860–1942) and Sir Leslie Ward (1851–1922), the celebrated 'Spy' of *Vanity Fair*, who continued in a slightly less robust form till 1914. The great criticism of the magazine (certainly after Pellegrini's death) was that it was no longer publishing caricatures but rather flattering portraits. The 'Nineties were, after all, a period of the beautifully crafted stiletto rather than the crude hatchet, and one would have expected the epicene decadents of *The Yellow Book* to be viewed accordingly.

Beerbohm contributed to *Vanity Fair* in 1896 and again at a later date, but clearly preferred more independent journals. In the years immediately following his début and in the few years after 1900, Beerbohm depicted the whole of his charmed circle with wit and sympathy, only rarely with asperity. In these caricatures, the most delightful and the most evocative of the vanished *fin de siècle*, the whole parade of artists, men of letters, men about town, politicians and dandies passes before our eyes. Sometimes they come singly, sometimes in pairs, less usually in groups like the celebrated 'Some Persons of The Nineties' in which he features himself. He knows each personality through and through, and elicits from them in a few words of explanation, a perfect literary or aesthetic image, just as his few lines elicit a perfect synthesis of the physiognomy.

Aubrey Beardsley appears in five caricatures between 1894 and 1896, Charles Conder in two; Charles Ricketts and Charles Shannon could hardly escape that penetrating eye, neither could William Rothenstein, James Pryde nor Phil May. There is Herbert Horne of the *Hobby Horse*, William Strang of the powerful etchings, Oscar Wilde in numerous guises, and Henry Tonks, J. S. Sargent and Philip Wilson Steer. Surprisingly there are some lesser figure of the art world like S. H. Sime, Walter Russell and Albert Rutherston, but one naturally expects illustrators like Joseph Pennell to be included. Sturge Moore appears in two caricatures and Mortimer Menpes in one; Henry Harland, the editor of *The Yellow Book* in no less than four. There are Harry Furniss, the *Punch* cartoonist, William de Gleyn and Charle Furse, the artists, and Comyns Carr, editor of the *English Illustrated Magazine*. Max Beerbohm himself was the great survivor; he went on drawing these men of the 'Nineties for years, almost as if he cherished their presences and mourned their period.

Beerbohm also succeeded at this time in creating something that was practically a new genre, the album of literary or aesthetic caricatures based upon fact. In November 1901, Robert Ross, then running the Carfax Gallery in Ryder Street, London, gave Max a one-man show including the series of cartoons known as 'The Second Childhood of John Bull' chronicling the ugly side of British politics. These were not very good; as a recent biographer put it, 'His line lacks the strength to convey savagery'.[15] This was followed shortly afterwards by the brilliant album book, *The Poet's Corner*, published by Heinemann in 1904. Here he explores the most celebrated figures of the nineteenth century, gently poking fun in word and sketch at Byron, Wordsworth, Ibsen, Tennyson, Arnold and Verlaine and even including Shakespeare. It is very much a production of the 'Nineties, reflecting the irreverent attitude to literary reputations, even the greatest literary reputations, and the brittle chat of the salons pierced by Beardsley's falsetto laughs. Almost the last cartoon in *The Poet's Corner* is 'Dante Gabriel Rossetti in His Back Garden', a witty gathering of all the chief Pre-Raphaelite figures including Morris, Swinburne, Elizabeth

'Some Persons of "The Nineties" Little Imagining, Despite their Proper Pride and Ornamental Aspect, How Much They Will Interest Mr. Holbrook Jackson And Mr. Osbert Burdett' by Max Beerbohm (1872–1956).
(Ashmolean Museum)

Siddal and Ruskin. This was the first idea for Beerbohm's celebrated book, *Rossetti and His Circle*, not published until 1922 and, in one sense, the last book of the 'Nineties. The artist gathered material from photographs and anecdotes from survivors of the movement to present scenes of historical caricature, a completely new dimension for the art.

Max's caricatures are a better index to the *fin de siècle* than any memoirs, although they do not explain the strange conundrums of their subjects. The illustrators of the 'Nineties were more French than English in their aspirations and yet they were oddly subservient to unaesthetic laws of economics, the art of both Beardsley and May being partly the result of the line block. There was no single credo, the 'art for art's sake' of the earlier days being blurred by symbolism, the Arts and Crafts, *art nouveau*, revivalism, anarchism and socialism. 'Great thoughts, great emotions were lacking', William Gaunt wrote. 'To the prophet and the reformer there succeeded the wit and the outcast, and the exhortations of the preacher were followed by the mockery of the *enfant terrible*.'[16] Paradoxically, in the midst of this maelstrom, the artists succeeded in reaching heights that they could hardly have believed possible. In a period that loved colour, the illustrators achieved a mastery of black-and-white that has never been surpassed since. At a period of rampant commercialism, the designers of books created more lavish and better crafted volumes than ever before. The *fin de siècle* remained, and remains, the enigma that contemporaries felt it to be. Perhaps the last word should be given to an illustrator and writer, W. Graham Robertson. 'The 'Nineties were to me a wonderful period,' he wrote, 'The century was dying bravely in no dreary winter of old age but in what seemed a burst of late summer, sunny and fair, though flowers were beginning to fall. But with the end of the decade came war, unrest, in the air was a vague note of change, faint yet perceptible.'[17]

Notes

CHAPTER ONE

1. *The Yellow Book*, Vol. 5, p. 278
2. ibid. p. 279
3. W. Gaunt, *The Aesthetic Adventure*, 1945, p. 113
4. W. Rothenstein, *Men and Memories*, 1931, Vol. 1, p. 69
5. W. Crane, *The Decorative Illustration of Books*, 1901, p. 161
6. Christopher Dresser's book was published in London and New York; Sir Robert Edis's work embraced very broad principles.
7. Quoted in R. McMullen, *Victorian Outsider*, 1973, p. 235
8. Leslie Bailey, *The Gilbert and Sullivan Book*, 1953, p. 189
9. Hans Brill, ed., *The Art Press*, Art Book Company, 1976, p. 24
10. J. Lewis May, *John Lane and the 90s*, 1936, p. 39
11. E.R. Pennell, *The Life and Letters of Joseph Pennell*, 1930, Vol. 1, p. 295
12. ibid. p. 297
13. A.S. Hartrick, *A Painter's Pilgrimage Through Fifty Years*, 1939, p. 115

CHAPTER TWO

1. J. Pennell, *Modern Illustration*, 1895, p. 103
2. *A Catalogue of Books From The Library of The Late Gleeson White*, 1899, pp. *viii–ix*
3. Clive Ashwin, 'Gleeson White, Aesthete & Editor', *Apollo*, October 1978, pp. 256–61
4. May, op. cit., p. 34
5. *The Pageant*, 1896, p. 81
6. ibid. p. 80
7. ibid. pp. 74–81
8. Rothenstein, op. cit., Vol. 1, p. 175
9. Printed exhibition catalogue in the R. de Beaumont Collection
10. ibid.
11. *Moxon Tennyson*, 1901, edited by J. Pennell, pp. *xiv–xv*
12. Laurence Housman, *The Unexpected Years*, 1937, p. 112
13. Laurence Housman, *Arthur Boyd Houghton*, 1896, p. 17
14. ibid. p. 28
15. Hartrick, op. cit., p. 3
16. Charles Holmes, *Self and Partners*, 1936, p. 132
17. Housman, op. cit., *The Unexpected Years*, p. 115
18. ibid. p. 120
19. ibid. p. 118
20. Laurence Housman, 'Pre-Raphaelitism in Art and Poetry', *Essays By Divers Hands*, R.S.L., 1933, Vol. XII, p. 12
21. Housman, op. cit., 'Pre-Raphaelitism. . .', p. 16
22. Crane, op. cit., p. 218
23. An inscribed copy of Arnold's *Poems* from Ospovat to Way was in the collection of R. de Beaumont.
24. Oliver Onions, *The Works of Henry Ospovat*, 1911, p. 11
25. Housman, op. cit., *The Unexpected Years*, p. 110
26. J.P. Cole, *Herbert Cole, a Brief Survey*, Nottingham 1985, p. 15
27. ibid. p. 30
28. R. Vicat Cole, *The Art and Life of Byam Shaw*, 1932, p. 72
29. J.M. Bulloch, 'Modern Pen Drawings, European and American', *The Studio*, Special Winter Number, 1900–1, p. 42

CHAPTER THREE

1. J. Pennell, op. cit., *Modern Illustration*, pp. 98–9
2. Gleeson White, 'The Work of Charles Ricketts', *The Pageant*, 1896, p. 84
3. Letter to Norton, 20 November 1894, Pierpont Morgan Library
4. Crane, op. cit., p. 208
5. Walter Crane, *An Artist's Reminiscences*, 1907, p. 328
6. Aymer Vallance, *William Morris, His Art, His Writings & His Public Life*, 1897, p. 394
7. Crane, op. cit. *An Artist's Reminiscences*, p. 429
8. Aymer Vallance, op. cit., pp. 389–90
9. May Morris, *W. Morris, Artist, Writer, Socialist*, Oxford 1936, Vol. 1, p. 318
10. E.R. Pennell, op. cit., *Life and Letters*, Vol. 1, pp. 218–9
11. Crane, op. cit., *Decorative Illustration*, p. 203
12. *The Studio*, Vol. 2, 1893, p. 110
13. ibid.
14. Crane, op. cit., *Decorative Illustration*, p. 203
15. *The Studio*, Vol. 4, 1894, p. xx
16. ibid.
17. ibid.
18. *A. & G. Gaskin*, catalogue of exhibition, City Museum & Art Gallery, Birmingham, 1982, Pl.110
19. Crane, op. cit., *Decorative Illustration*, p. 203
20. May, op. cit., p. 209
21. Rothenstein, op. cit., Vol. 1, p. 34
22. Holmes, op. cit., p. 149
23. Rothenstein, op. cit., Vol. 1, p. 34

CHAPTER FOUR

1. J. Pennell, op. cit., *Modern Illustration*, p. 115
2. E.R. Pennell, op. cit., *Life and Letters*, p. 138
3. ibid. p. 218
4. E.V. Lucas, *Edwin Austin Abbey*, 1921, Vol. 1, p. 110
5. E.R. Pennell, op. cit., *Life and Letters*, Vol. 1, p. 218
6. Rothenstein, op. cit., Vol. 1, p. 44
7. Crane, op. cit., *Decorative Illustration*, p. 165.
8. ibid. p. 166
9. Ashwin, op. cit., p. 258
10. *The Studio*, Vol. 1, 1893, pp. 143–9
11. E.R. Pennell, op. cit., *Life and Letters*, Vol. 1, p. 217
12. ibid. p. 248
13. Alfred Thornton, *The Diary of an Art Student of the Nineties*, 1938, p. 38
14. J. Pennell, *Pen Drawing and Pen Draughtsmen*, 1895, p. 226
15. Harry Furniss, *Confessions of a Caricaturist*, 1901, pp. 405–7
16. Bulloch, op. cit., p. 88
17. *The Studio*, Vol. 2, 1893, p. 114
18. ibid. Vol. 7, 1895, pp. 188–9
19. ibid.
20. I have seen direct copies from Gibson's albums by these two artists.
21. May, op. cit., p. 152
22. ibid.
23. J. Pennell, op. cit., *Pen Drawing*, p. 232
24. J. Pennell, op. cit., *Modern Illustration*, p. 94
25. *The Studio*, Vol. 4, 1894, p. 167
26. ibid.
27. C. Lewis Hind, *Napthali*, 1926, p. 89
28. *Modern Illustration*, catalogue of an exhibition at the Victoria and Albert Museum, 1900–1, 2nd edition

CHAPTER FIVE

1. Hind, op. cit., p. 62
2. *The Studio*, Vol. 1, 1893, p. 14
3. *The Studio*, Vol. 2. 1893, p. 183
4. ibid.
5. Robert Ross, *Aubrey Beardsley*, 1909, p. 43
6. Crane, op. cit., *Decorative Illustration*, p. 221
7. *The Studio*, Vol. 2, 1893, p. 185
8. Ross, op. cit., p. 45
9. ibid. p. 39
10. D. S. Macoll, *Le Monde Artiste*, reprinted in *A Beardsley Miscellany*, R. A. Walker, 1949, p. 25
11. Rothenstein, op. cit., Vol. 1, p. 135
12. D. S. Macoll, op. cit., p. 27
13. *The Idler*, Vol. IX, 1897, p. 192
14. R. Halsband, *The Rape of The Lock and Its Illustrators*, 1980, p. 106
15. *The Savoy*, January 1896

16. Ross, op. cit., p. 49
17. *Apollo*, October 1973, p. 262
18. Hind, op. cit., p. 87
19. *The Idler*, Vol XIII, 1898, p. 540
20. *The Studio*, Special Winter Number, 1900–1, p. 160
21. Ross, op. cit., p. 41
22. *The Idler*, op. cit., p. 544

CHAPTER SIX

1. May, op. cit., p. 122–3
2. Rothenstein, op. cit., Vol. 1, p. 336
3. G. Deghy and K. Waterhouse, *Café Royal, Ninety Years of Bohemia*, 1956, p. 61
4. Rothenstein, op. cit., Vol. 1, p. 188
5. Hind, op. cit., p. 88
6. May, op. cit., p. 74
7. K. Beckson, *Henry Harland: His Life & Work*, 1978, p. 69
8. *The Yellow Book*, Vol. 2, p. 186
9. ibid. p. 188
10. W. Graham Robertson, *Time Was*, 1931, p. 130
11. *The Savoy*, December 1896, p. 92
12. James Thorpe, *English Illustration, The Nineties*, 1935, p. 173
13. ibid. p. 174
14. Bernard Muddiman, *The Men of the Nineties*, 1920, p. 121
15. James Thorpe, op. cit., p. 195
16. Rothenstein, op. cit., p. 226
17. ibid. p. 60–1

CHAPTER SEVEN

1. C. S. Felver, *Joseph Crawhall, The Newcastle Wood-Engraver 1821–1896*, 1972, pp. 94–5
2. E. Gordon Craig, *Woodcuts and Some Words*, 1924, p. 8
3. E. Gordon Craig, *Index to the Story of My Days*, 1956, p. 214
4. ibid. p. 191
5. Rothenstein, op. cit., Vol. 1, p. 277
6. ibid. p. 302
7. Craig, op. cit., *Index*, p. 206
8. Craig, op. cit., *Woodcuts*, p. 99
9. *The Studio*, Vol. 15, 1899, p. 210
10. ibid. Vol. 18, 1900, p. 218
11. ibid. Vol. 21, 1900, p. 210
12. Craig, op. cit., *Woodcuts*, p. 8
13. H. Davray and J. Laver, *XIXth Century French Posters*, 1944, p. 17
14. F. L. Emanuel, *Illustrators of Montmartre*, 1904, p. 84
15. Alfred Munnings, *An Artist's Life*, 1950, p. 97
16. James Thorpe, *Phil May*, 1932, p. 28
17. Rothenstein, op. cit., p. 57

18. ibid. p. 58
19. Thorpe, op. cit., *May*, p. 97
20. M. H. Spielmann, *The History of Punch*, 1895, p. 569
21. E. R. Pennell, op. cit., *Life and Letters*, Vol. 1, p. 249
22. Emanuel, op. cit., p. 68
23. A. E. Johnson, *John Hassall*, Brush, Pen and Pencil, 1913, p. 20
24. A. E. Johnson, *Tom Browne*, Brush, Pen and Pencil, 1909, pp. 3–4
25. E. J. Sullivan, *The Art of Illustration*, 1921, pp. 106–7
26. ibid. p. 219
27. Colin Franklin, *The Private Presses*, 1969, p. 93

CHAPTER EIGHT

1. *The Studio*, Special Winter Number, 1897–8, p. 34
2. ibid. p. 59
3. ibid. p. 40
4. Thomas Balston, 'English Book Illustration 1880–1900', *New Paths in Book Collecting*, ed. J. Carter, 1934, p. 178
5. *The Studio*, Special Winter Number, 1897–8, p. 46
6. ibid. p. 59
7. *The Studio*, Vol. 7, 1895, p. 36
8. ibid. pp. 146–50
9. *The Studio*, Special Winter Number, 1897–8, p. 60
10. Crane, op. cit., *Decorative Illustration*, p. 223
11. May, op. cit., p. 208
12. Crane, op. cit., *Decorative Illustration*, p. 223.
13. *The Studio*, Special Winter Number, 1897–8, p. 47
14. J.M. Dent, *The House of Dent 1888–1938*, p. 68
15. ibid. p. 69
16. Sotheby's, 19 June 1987, 2 December 1988, 8 June 1990
17. *The Studio*, Special Winter Number, 1897–8, p. 60
18. ibid. p. 59
19. Dent, op. cit., p. 113
20. Sotheby's, op. cit.
21. Charles Morgan, *The House of Macmillan*, 1941, p. 189
22. Letter from Hugh Thomson to Macmillan, 18 March 1894, British Library
23. Rothenstein, op. cit., p. 137

CHAPTER NINE

1. Crane, op. cit., *Modern Illustration*, p. 106.
2. Simon Houfe, *John Leech and The Victorian Scene*, 1984, p. 192.
3. *The Studio*, Special Winter Number, 1897–8, p. 38
4. G. A. Sala, 'William Hogarth, Painter, Engraver & Philosopher, Essays on The Man, The Work and The Time', *Cornhill Magazine*, March to November 1860. Published as *William Hogarth*, 1866
5. Linley Sambourne to Macmillan, 27 March 1883, British Library
6. Michael Hutchins, editor, *Yours Pictorially*, Illustrated Letters of Randolph Caldecott, 1976
7. Balston, op. cit., p. 167
8. Linley Sambourne to Macmillan, 28 November 1886, British Library
9. Hugh Thomson to Macmillan, 28 March 1891, British Library
10. Hugh Thomson to Macmillan, 18 March 1894, British Library
11. Hugh Thomson to Macmillan, 10 April 1898, British Library
12. C. E. Brock to Macmillan, 7 November 1894, British Library
13. Balston, op. cit., p. 174
14. Thorpe, op. cit., p. 148
15. Percy V. Bradshaw, *The Art of The Illustrator: E. J. Sullivan*, 1916
16. James Thorpe, *E. J. Sullivan*, 1948, p. 25
17. *The Studio*, Vol. 4, 1894, p. 95
18. A sketch-book for *Sartor Resartus* was in the Gordon Ray Collection; *The Illustrator and The Book in England*, 1976, p. 188
19. Bradshaw, op. cit., p. 4
20. ibid. p. 5
21. Rothenstein, op. cit., p. 177
22. ibid. p. 184
23. ibid. p. 344

CHAPTER TEN

1. *The Studio*, Special Winter Number, 1898–9, p. 6
2. ibid. pp. 14–5
3. ibid. p. 14
4. ibid. p. 20
5. ibid. p. 24
6. ibid. p. 25
7. ibid. p. 40
8. Brian North Lee, *British Book Plates, A Pictorial History*, 1979, p. 104
9. Simon Houfe, 'Lured by Rural Roots', *Country Life*, 21 March 1991
10. *The Studio*, Special Winter Number, 1894, p. 42
11. W. Shaw Sparrow, *Memories of Life and Art*, 1925, pp. 249–50
12. Leonee Ormond, *George du Maurier*, 1969, p. 428
13. ibid. p. 463
14. David Cecil, *Max a biography*, 1964, p. 57
15. ibid. p. 179
16. Gaunt, op. cit., p. 216
17. Graham Robertson, op. cit., p. 287

Frontispiece by J. J. Guthrie (1874–1952) for *Art and Nature
Sonnets* by Osmaston, 1900.

Bibliography

GENERAL

Amaya, M., *Art Nouveau*, 1966

Balston, T., 'Illustrated Series of the Nineties', *Book Collectors Quarterly*, Vol. 3, 1933

Brill, H., editor, *The Art Press*, Art Book Company, 1976

Davray, H. and Laver, J., *XIXth Century French Posters*, 1944

Deghy, G. and Waterhouse, K., *Café Royal, Ninety Years of Bohemia*, 1956

Dent, J.M., *The House of Dent 1888–1938*, 1938

Emanuel, F.L., *Illustrators of Montmartre*, 1904

Franklin, C., *The Private Presses*, 1969

Gaunt, W., *The Aesthetic Adventure*, 1945

Halsband, R., *The Rape of The Lock and Its Illustrators*, 1980

Hind, C.L., *Naphtali*, 1926

Holmes, C., *Self and Partners*, 1936

Houfe, S., *Dictionary of British Book Illustrators and Caricaturists 1800–1914*, 1978

Johnson, Diana L. and Landow, G.P., *Fantastic Illustration and Design in Britain 1850–1930*, exhibition catalogue, Rhode Island School of Design, Cooper-Hewitt Museum, 1979

Lee, B.N., *British Book Plates, A Pictorial History*, 1979

May, J.L., *John Lane and the 90s*, 1936

Morgan, C., *The House of Macmillan*, 1941

Muddiman, B., *The Men of The Nineties*, 1920

Muir, P., *Victorian Illustrated Books*, 1971

Muir, P., *English Children's Books*, 1954

Pennell, J., *Modern Illustration*, 1895

Pennell, J., *Pen Drawing and Pen Draughtsmen*, 1895

Peppin, B. and Mickelthwait, L., *Dictionary of British Book Illustrators, The Twentieth Century*, 1983

Ray, G.N., *The Illustrator and The Book in England*, Pierpont Morgan Library, 1976

Ray, G.N., *The Art of The French Illustrated Book 1700–1914*, Pierpont Morgan Library, 1982

Rothenstein, W., *Men and Memories*, 3 Vols, 1931–3

Sketchley, R.E.D., *English Book Illustration of Today*, 1903

Sparrow, W. Shaw, *Memories of Life and Art*, 1925

Spencer, R., *The Aesthetic Movement*, 1972

Spielmann, M.H., *The History of Punch*, 1895

Studio, Special Winter Number, 1896–7, 'Childrens' Books'

Studio, Special Winter Number, 1897–8, 'British Book Plates'

Studio, Special Winter Number, 1900–1, 'Modern Pen Drawings, European and American'

Taylor, J.R., *The Art Nouveau Book in Britain*, 1966

Thornton, A., *The Diary of an Art Student of the Nineties*, 1938

Thorpe, J., *English Illustration, The Nineties*, 1935

Wheatley, Henry B., ed., catalogue of exhibition, *Modern Illustration*, Victoria and Albert Museum, 1900–1

White, G., *English Illustration, The Sixties*, 1897

INDIVIDUAL ARTISTS

Calloway, S., *Charles Ricketts, Subtle and Fantastic Decorator*, 1979

Campbell, C., *The Beggarstaff Posters*, 1990

Campbell, C., *William Nicholson: The Graphic Work*, 1992

Cecil, D., *Max a biography*, 1964

Christian, J., ed., *The Last Romantics*, The Romantic Tradition in British Art, catalogue of exhibition at the Barbican Gallery, 1989

Beare, G., *The Illustrations of W. Heath Robinson*, 1983

Cole, J.P., *Herbert Cole, a Brief Survey*, Nottingham, 1985 (privately printed)

Cole, R.V., *The Art and Life of Byam Shaw*, 1932

Craig, E.G., *Index to the Story of My Days*, 1956

Crane, W. *An Artist's Reminiscences*, 1907

Darracott, J., *The World of Charles Ricketts*, 1980

Delaney, J.G.P., *Charles Ricketts*, 1989

Emmons, R., *The Life and Opinions of Robert William Sickert*, 1941

Felver, C.S., *Joseph Crawhall, The Newcastle Wood-Engraver 1821–1896*, 1972

de Freitas, L., *Charles Robinson*, 1976

Furniss, H., *Confessions of a Caricaturist*, 1901

Gaskin, A. & G., catalogue of exhibiton, City Museum and Art Gallery, Birmingham, 1982

Hart-Davis, R., ed., *A Catalogue of the Caricatures of Max Beerbohm*, 1972

Hartrick, A.S., *A Painter's Pilgrimage Through Fifty Years*, 1939

Hind, C.L., *The Uncollected Work of Aubrey Beardsley*, 1925

Housman, L., *Arthur Boyd Houghton*, 1896

Housman, L., *The Unexpected Years*, 1937

Housman: *Catalogue of the Ian Kenyur-Hodgkins Collection of Laurence Housman*, Church Enstone, 1978

Hutchins, M., ed., *Yours Pictorially*, Illustrated Letters of Randolph Caldecott, 1976

Johnson, A.E., *Tom Browne*, Brush, Pen and Pencil Series, 1909

Johnson, A.E., *John Hassall*, Brush, Pen and Pencil Series, 1913

Lucas, E.V., *Edwin Austin Abbey*, 2 Vols, 1921

McMullen, R., *Victorian Outsider*, A Biography of J.A.M. Whistler, 1973

Morris, M., *William Morris, Artist, Writer, Socialist*, 2 Vols, 1936

Munnings, A.J., *An Artist's Life*, 1950

Nicholson, K., Introduction, *Kay Nielsen*, 1975

Onions, O., *The Works of Henry Ospovat*, 1911

Ormond, L., *George du Maurier*, 1969

Pennell, E.R., *The Life and Letters of Joseph Pennell*, 2 Vols, 1930

Read, Brian, *Beardsley*, 1967

Robertson, W. Graham, *Time Was*, 1931

Robinson, D., *William Morris, Edward Burne-Jones and the Kelmscott Chaucer*, 1982

Ross, R., *Aubrey Beardsley*, 1909

Rothenstein, J., *The Life and Death of Conder*, 1938

Thorold, Anne, *Lucien Pissarro: His Influence on English Art 1890–1914*, Canterbury Museum, 1986

Taylor, G., *Centenary Exhibition of Works By Eleanor Fortescue Brickdale 1872–1945*, Ashmolean Museum catalogue, 1972–3

Thorpe, J., *Phil May*, 1932

Thorpe, J., *E.J. Sullivan*, 1948

Vallance, A., *William Morris, His Art, His Writings & His Public Life*, 1897

Walker, R.A., *A Beardsley Miscellany*, 1949

TECHNICAL

Bradshaw, P.V., *E.J. Sullivan*, The Art of The Illustrator, 1916

Bradshaw, P.V., *Bernard Partridge*, The Art of The Illustrator, 1916

Bradshaw, P.V., *F.H. Townsend*, The Art of The Illustrator, 1916

Bradshaw, P.V., *C.E. Brock*, The Art of The Illustrator, 1916

Craig, E.G., *Woodcuts and Some Words*, 1924

Crane, W., *The Decorative Illustration of Books*, 1901

Sullivan, E.J., *Line, an Art Study*, 1921

Sullivan, E.J., *The Art of Illustration*, 1922

Wakeman, G., *Victorian Book Illustration — The Technical Revolution*, 1973

COLLECTIONS

Aberdeen Art Gallery: The collection contains works by R. Anning Bell, Frank Brangwyn, Robert Burns, James Cadenhead, Charles Conder, Walter Crane, George du Maurier, John Duncan, J.L. Forain, James Pryde, Walter Sickert, Wilson Steer, William Strang and Hugh Thomson.

Bedford, Cecil Higgins Art Gallery: Important works by Aubrey Beardsley, Charles Conder, George du Maurier, Phil May, Lucien Pissarro and Charles Ricketts.

Birmingham City Art Gallery: Most of the Birmingham School are represented here including A.J. Gaskin, C.M. Gere and Joseph Southall. In addition, there are important works by J.D. Batten and Eleanor Fortescue Brickdale and many drawings by the 1860s illustrators who inspired them.

Bradford Art Gallery: Good works by R. Anning Bell and Charles Ricketts.

Cambridge, Fitzwilliam Museum: The museum contains the important Ricketts and Shannon bequest including many drawings by their contemporaries. Works by Ricketts and Shannon themselves, Walter Crane and E.J. Detmold, and one of the finest groups of drawings by Sir Edward Burne-Jones for the Kelmscott books.

Carlisle Art Gallery: This gallery contains the important Gordon Bottomley Collection featuring many works of the '90s. Among them are drawings by Clinton Balmer, Thomas Sturge Moore, May Morris, William Morris, Charles Ricketts (including an album of drawings) and W. Graham Robertson.

Coventry, Herbert Art Gallery: Some work by Charles Ricketts.

Derby City Art Gallery: Some work by Charles Ricketts.

Dundee Art Gallery: Works by John Duncan.

Edinburgh, National Galleries of Scotland: Work by John Duncan.

Glasgow City Art Gallery: Works by E.A. Hornel.

Glasgow, Glasgow University Collection: Works by Aubrey Beardsley, Alexandre Steinlen and Félix Vallotton. Important collections of Charles Rennie Mackintosh (including graphics), Frances and Margaret Macdonald and Herbert Nacnair. The gallery contains the Birnie Philip Collection of Whistler's works, one of the most comprehensive in existence.

Liverpool, Walker Art Gallery: Work by Eleanor Fortescue Brickdale, C.M. Gere, William Russell Flint, C.H. Shannon and others.

London, British Museum: Works by J.D. Batten, Walter Crane, Edmund Dulac, George du Maurier, C.M. Gere, Kate Greenaway, J.J. Guthrie, Phil May, T. Sturge Moore, William Morris, George Morrow, Arthur Rackham, Charles Ricketts, W. Graham Robertson, W. Heath Robinson, W. Russell Flint, C.H. Shannon, William Strang and E.J. Sullivan.

London, Tate Gallery: Works by Aubrey Beardsley, R. Anning Bell, Laurence Housman, Charles Ricketts, C.H. Shannon, J. Southall and others.

London, Victoria and Albert Museum: Works by E.A. Abbey, Cecil Aldin, Aubrey Beardsley, E. Gordon Craig, Walter Crane, George du Maurier, H.J. Ford, Cyril Goldie, Maurice Greiffenhagen, J.J. Guthrie, John Hassall, Charles Ricketts, C.H. Shannon and others. The collection includes the Ingram Bequest, 1914, and the Harrod Bequest, 1948, containing many '90s illustrations, some by minor artists.

London, Linley Sambourne House, 18 Stafford Terrace, W.8: The home of the *Punch* artist contains many drawings by Linley Sambourne and his contemporaries.

Manchester City Art Gallery: Works by J.D. Batten; Charles Ricketts, C.H. Shannon and others.

Newcastle-upon-Tyne, Laing Art Gallery: Works by Tom Browne, Sir Edward Burne-Jones, Dudley Hardy, Selwyn Image, Charles Ricketts, W. Rothenstein, Albert Rutherston and Frank Brangwyn.

Preston, Harris Museum and Art Gallery: Works by E.A. Abbey.

U.S.A.

Harvard University, Fogg Art Museum: A very important collection of Aubrey Beardsley's drawings, including the *Salome* series and rare late works.

Princeton University Library: An important collection of Aubrey Beardsley's drawings, including early works.

Index

Acknowledgements

In the preparation of this book I have received much generous help and advice from many friends and collectors. I would especially like to thank all those who have let me examine drawings and books in their possession, and kindly allowed me to reproduce the drawings in this survey of the 'Nineties. Every effort has been made to obtain the necessary permission with reference to copyright material; should there be any omissions in this respect, I apologise and shall be pleased to make the appropriate acknowledgement in any future edition.

I owe a deep debt to Robin de Beaumont who has given me great assistance, not only with his unrivalled knowledge of the subject, but also by making suggestions and giving me full access to his matchless library. I have also been fortunate in being able to borrow material from two other private collections through the courtesy of the Trustees of the Sir Albert Richardson Collection and of Mrs Stonborough.

My thanks go to Sir Rupert Hart-Davis for allowing me to reproduce a cartoon by Max Beerbohm, to Mrs Elizabeth Banks — the works of the Beggarstaffs and William Nicholson are reproduced by kind permission of Elizabeth Banks — and to the Hon. Mrs Alice

Winn for showing me works by her uncle, Charles Dana Gibson.

The following individuals have greatly helped me with my researches: Phillip Athill (Abbott & Holder), Chris Beetles (Chris Beetles Gallery, St James's, London), Michael Broadbent (Christie's), Stephen Callaway, Dr Colin Campbell, John Christian, Amanda Jane Doran (*Punch*), Rodney Enghen (Maas Gallery), Lady Graham (Cecil Higgins Art Gallery, Bedford), Michael Heseltine (Sotheby's), Derek Hudson, Professor E.D.G. Johnson, Lionel Lambourne (Victoria & Albert Museum), Charles Sebag-Montefiore, Countess F. Stampa Gruss, Dr Catharine Whistler (Ashmolean Museum), Stephen Wildman (Birmingham City Art Gallery), David Wootton (Chris Beetles Gallery, St James's, London).

I have had unfailing help from the Ashmolean Museum, Birmingham City Art Gallery, Christie's New York, Albert Sloman Library, University of Essex, London Library, Victoria & Albert Picture Library, and the Victoria & Albert Library.

Lastly, I am very grateful to Sarah Finch who read the proofs.